Making the Most of Being a Student

The Daily Telegraph

LIFEPLANNER

Making the Most of Being a Student

Judy
Bastyra

Charles
Bradley

**KOGAN
PAGE**

YOURS TO HAVE AND TO HOLD
BUT NOT TO COPY

First published in 1998

Kogan Page Limited
120 Pentonville Road
London N1 9JN

British Library Cataloguing in Publication Data

A CIP record for this book is available from the British Library.

ISBN 0 7494 2641 1

Typeset by Kogan Page Ltd
Printed and bound in Great Britain by Clays Ltd, St Ives plc

Contents

The Lifeplanner Series

There are many situations in life for which your education, your parents or your experience simply have not prepared you. In this major new series, Kogan Page and *The Daily Telegraph* have joined forces with a team of expert writers to provide practical, down-to-earth information and advice for anyone encountering such a situation for the first time.

The series addresses personal finance and consumer issues in a jargon-free, readable way, taking the fear out of planning your life. So whether you are thinking about buying a house, having a baby or just deciding what to spend your first pay cheque on, the Lifeplanner series will help you do so wisely.

Titles available are:

The Young Professional's Guide to Personal Finance
Your First Home: A Practical Guide to Buying and Renting
Making the Most of Being a Student

Forthcoming titles are:

Balancing Your Career, Family and Life
Your First Investment Portfolio
Your Child's Education

Available from all good booksellers. For further information on the series, please contact:

Kogan Page
120 Pentonville Road
London
N1 9JN
Tel: 0171 278 0433
Fax: 0171 837 6348
e-mail: kpinfo@kogan-page.co.uk

Acknowledgements

We would like to thank the following people and organizations for helping us to research this book:

Lola Almudevar, Luke Arthur, Pippa Bagnall, Gaby Bastyra, Nell Battie, Professor Katherine Castle, Gemma Crossingham, Pete Davis, Pepsi Denning, Gill Driver, Kate Joseph, Katie Lee, Maureen Lipman, Caroline Mandy, Barney Myers, Chris Reeve, Amy Rosenthal, Clare Spurrell, Caroline Virr, Andy Wiley and Lisa Wood. With particular thanks to the National Union of Students, the University of North London and the hundreds of students around the country who participated in our survey of student life. We would also like to thank Vicky Unwin and Sue Pollock for their support.

This book is dedicated to Dominic and Gaby – please read it carefully!

Introduction

Making The Most of Being a Student has been written for students making that big leap from school to higher education. It is often said that your school days are the best years of your life, but we dispute that. Your time at university can be some of the best years too.

The aims of this book are to help you to find your way through your degree years as easily as possible and to help you to make the most of the opportunities available to you.

University is not just about studying for your degree. There are many other skills that you will learn as well: how to manage your finances, how to look after yourself and your health, how to make decisions, how to study on your own and at the same time how to enjoy your new independence.

All the problems that confront you have been faced by countless students over the years; but they will still be new to you. We hope this book will make the path easier for you and lead to success in your studies as well as fulfilment in your social life.

1 Accommodation: A Roof Over Your Head

I just can't wait to leave home and get my own space.

It's January. You are sitting in the warmth of the parental home fretting about your A-levels. Two universities have made you an offer and all you seem to be able to think about is whether you can turn that predicted 'C' into a 'B'.

But it is worth taking a few moments to study the prospectuses you've received. Most universities will send you information about the accommodation that they offer, along with a map showing the locations of various key parts of the institute and the application form for accommodation.

It is a good idea to apply for accommodation – particularly for halls of residence – at the same time as you are offered a place at the university.

> *One thing I would say is pretty important is: if you are interested in halls of residence don't leave it to the last minute. Contact us as soon as possible. You need to get yourself sorted out. A lot of people believe that there's no point in applying for halls until their results come through. What they don't know is that if they wait until their results come through they will have missed out. If they apply before their results come through but don't get the grades, they can notify us that they can't come. Basically we start our allocation process from June. (Accommodation Officer, University of North London)*

If you don't make your grades, you can always cancel. Someone who applied later will be very grateful.

Open Days

It is also useful, if you can, to visit the university for an open day and get a good idea of where everything is located in relation to everything else. There are normally several dates when you can visit, some of which may be for specific departments only. A student will be assigned to show you around. Some student accommodation may be just next to your faculty but miles away from any shops or pubs, whereas the halls may be nearer the centre of town and only five minutes away from the faculty by bus or ten minutes by bike. To find out these kind of things, you might know someone who is already there, or you can ask the student who is showing you around. Certain halls of residence seem to attract certain types of students. Talk to them and get a feel for the place and the students that are there. Remember, you are potentially choosing your home for the next nine months.

Some Good Questions To Ask About Accommodation

▌ What's the transport like?

▌ How long does it take to get to the lecture halls from the hall of residence or flat?

▌ Is there a good supermarket nearby?

▌ What's the food like in the halls?

▌ Are there good cheap places to eat nearby?

▌ Do you like living in halls?

▌ What are the best bars and pubs to go to?

▌ Will I need a bike?

▌ What's the best time to move in? (If you arrive at your student flat first you will be able to choose which room you have.)

▮   What sort of student does the hall attract? (Some places have a lot of foreign and mature students, others have a reputation for attracting public school students.)

On the whole, student accommodation tends towards the basic – a typical room will be equipped with a bed, a desk and chair, a few shelves, a wardrobe and perhaps, a pin-board. There probably isn't much room for anything else. You might get more space in a converted property, but you won't get much more in the way of furniture.

Halls of Residence

Most, but not all, universities have halls of residence. Basically a hall of residence is accommodation that is owned or leased and run by the university. It may be a huge purpose-built concrete block or a converted building such as an old hotel, a nursing hostel or an attractive row of terraced houses. Some halls are single-sex (usually for women) whilst a lot of others are mixed, with each gender being placed on a different floor or corridor. Each hall of residence has a live-in Warden.

> *After seven years at an all-girls school I promptly moved into an all-girls hall. I chose it because it was small safe and pretty, much like my school, and I stayed for two years, despite realizing fairly quickly that it was a claustrophobic hothouse of hormones and hysteria.*

Types of Accommodation in Halls of Residence

Self-catering single

Accommodation in which one person occupies a study-bedroom but has access to a kitchen which is also used by other students. An example of this kind of accommodation is a traditional student room in a hall of residence where there are eight people to a corridor and one kitchen per corridor.

Self-catering shared

Similar to the above, except more than one person occupies the same study-bedroom.

Self-catering en-suite

One person occupies a study-bedroom that also includes both bath/shower and WC facilities, but not a kitchen – this is shared with others.

Part board

Accommodation which includes the provision of one meal a day, and could be single or shared.

Full board

Accommodation which includes the provision of at least two meals a day, and could be single or shared.

Flats

Self-catering accommodation in which students, whilst having their own study-bedroom, share washing and WC facilities and a communal living-space within the unit. The accommodation may be a self-contained block where only the residents can use the living-space.

Head tenancies

Accommodation rented by the institution from private landlords who have signed up to a designated scheme. The landlord is non-resident and the accommodation is then rented out to students by the institution. The reason for including this category within institutional accommodation is a perception amongst students that they are dealing with the college, and not a private individual. This category can also include properties owned by a housing association that is connected to the college/university.

Head lease

Halls or blocks of accommodation that an institution leases from another body such as an NHS Trust or local authority.

Other Alternatives

Youth Hostels

These should really only be considered as a temporary stopgap, as they are quite expensive and may have restrictive rules. They may, however, offer a short-term solution whilst you look for a flat or house to rent.

Bed and Breakfast

Once again, quite an expensive option, and you may have a formidable live-in landlady or landlord to contend with. Not recommended for undergraduates.

Student Hostels/Villages

Specially built areas catering for students' needs and quite popular on some campuses, especially the more isolated ones. The accommodation offered is much the same as in halls of residence, although usually self-catering.

Lodging with a Family or Landlady/Landlord

This can provide a good solution for someone leaving home for the first time and not quite confident enough to branch out on their own. You will be living with a family, however, and you will therefore be subject to their house rules, meal times, etc. One year in this sort of situation is usually enough for you to find your feet. You may also find yourself missing out on some aspects of University life.

Squatting

Some students may decide to set up a squat in an unoccupied property, but this is definitely not recommended. It may be a cheap solution, but the accommodation is usually pretty dire and someone will have to be in occupancy all the time to prevent the property being reclaimed. Whilst it is not illegal, the law has changed to make it easier for the owner to evict you. Once the court order has been obtained you could suddenly find yourself homeless, thrown out by the bailiffs. It is illegal to squat in Scotland.

Staying at Home

Of course, if you choose a local uni you can always stay right where you are – at home. It's certainly cheaper, cleaner, with better laundry facilities and great grub – but there's much less personal freedom and you miss the chance to experience and experiment with a new lifestyle.

Private Rented Accommodation

Looking for a Flat or House

If you've got a group of mates that you want to share with, you should all travel around and view the possible options together (this will avoid recriminations over a 'bad decision'). Alternatively, second- or third-year students may be looking for extra people to share a flat, or other first years who have not been placed in halls of residence may be looking for flatmates. Look at the notice boards around the campus and at the Students' Union, as well as advertising yourself. It is quite difficult to assess what people will be like to share with, but there is a better chance of it working out if you share some common interests and the same sort of study patterns. When you advertise write out:

▓ your age

- sex

- interests

- the course you are studying (it's better to live with people who have the same study pattern)

- how much you want to pay

- if you are a smoker

- any preferred area you want to live in

- how you can be contacted.

Be careful to check anyone who responds: ask to see their UCAS ID number.

Where to look for a flat

There are several ways to find out what flats are available to rent and what their market rental value is.

Your first point of inquiry should be the University Accommodation Office. They will have a list of landlords that they have vetted and found to be acceptable. However, the number of properties available is not limitless, so you may need to look elsewhere. You could try the following places:

- local press and free-ads papers

- newsagents' window

- estate or letting agent. If you find a property this way, you will need to pay an agent's fee when they find you somewhere to rent. This may be as much as a month's rent. On no account pay over any money before they have found you anywhere – this is illegal

- grapevine – from other students who have previously rented.

When you find a property that you like, go in with your eyes open. Look at the condition of the fabric of the building.

▌ Are there patches of damp? This will manifest itself by signs of staining, particularly around the bottom of the ground-floor walls, below the ceilings, around windows, in the bathroom or on the inside of walls with defective drainpipes or waste-pipes outside. But you don't need to be a chartered surveyor – if there is a problem you will be able to smell and feel the musty atmosphere.

▌ Are there signs of infestation from nasty wee creatures – mouse droppings, evidence of rat poison in the kitchen or slug trails around the door? Slugs are horrible to tread on with bare feet first thing in the morning.

▌ Do the windows fit properly? (You don't want a gale blowing through the house.)

▌ What is the security like on the doors and windows? (This is important for insurance as well.)

▌ Is there a smoke detector? Is there a means of escape in case of fire?

▌ What is the level of crime in the area? Does it feel safe for a single female? Visit the area in the evening and see what it feels like then.

▌ Do the appliances work? Don't be afraid to try things out – like the shower, cooker, loo, etc.

▌ What are the bills likely to be? Find out if you have to pay rent over the summer when you're not there.

▌ Is there central heating?

Don't sign a contract immediately – pay a small deposit and arrange to inspect the contract, talk about terms and have any repairs carried out before you move in.

Carbon Monoxide Safety

Make sure that the landlord can provide you with documented proof that all gas appliances and flues have been inspected within the previous twelve months by a CORGI gas engineer. Check that there is adequate ventilation where such appliances operate. There should be permanent ventilation, such as an airbrick or a louvre in the window, wherever there is a gas-operated appliance. Be careful to ensure that you aren't tempted to block them with that tasteful poster of the Teletubbies.

Ten students have died since 1991 from carbon monoxide poisoning. Carbon monoxide is a very dangerous odourless gas that makes you feel drowsy. If you experience headaches and nausea there may be a low but dangerous level. If you have any doubts you should contact the local Gas Board immediately, turn off the appliance, open the windows and go elsewhere.

You can buy detectors from DIY stores and some supermarkets quite cheaply.

Inventory

When you move into private rented accommodation you should draw up and agree an inventory with your landlord. An inventory is a list of all the contents of the property including their condition, as well as a description of the condition of the property itself (see Table 1.1). You should make sure that it is as detailed as possible (to avoid possible problems later on).

For example, if there is a handle missing from one of the cupboards, a huge stain on the carpet or a burn-mark on the work surface, you must note it, because if you don't you may very well be charged for damage to the property that was not your fault.

There should be at least two copies signed and dated by both you and the landlord, so that you each have one.

Table 1.1: Inventory

Inventory for 31B The Heights, Bingcaster, 27/9/98

Front door	Glass cracked Letter-box broken Four Yale keys and four mortice-lock keys
Hall and stairs	Carpet stained and frayed on first landing Two spindles missing on first flight Staining to ground-floor left wall
Sitting-room	Two armchairs, one stained with torn cushion One sofa Curtains do not close very easily Table surface scratched and stained Carpet worn by door Decor generally scruffy
Kitchen	Four dinner plates, all chipped Five mugs, one with missing handle Three bowls Seven side-plates, two chipped, one cracked Six teaspoons Fours knives Five forks Four spoons Two wooden spoons, one burnt Wooden breadboard, split Two saucepans, both dented Two saucepan lids, both dented One electric kettle One table, burnt in corner and marked with coffee rings Oven Fridge, one shelf missing Decor okay but quite stained
Bathroom	Towel-rail coming off wall

Three tiles cracked around bath
Carpet badly stained
Window, one pane cracked
Paintwork heavily discoloured.

Bedroom One   Wardrobe
Bed with stained mattress
Four blankets, one with several holes
Chair, slightly rickety
Carpet damaged in front of fireplace
Table
Decor good

Bedroom Two   Chest of drawers, bottom drawer broken top
     surface scratched
Wardrobe
Bed, headboard damaged
Four blankets, two stained
Two pillows
Carpet, stained by bed
Desk
Chair
Decor okay except stain to ceiling

Bedroom Three   Cupboard, one hinge broken
Bed
Four blankets
Two pillows
Carpet okay
Desk
Chair
Decor, several nail holes in wall. Door damaged
     with Sellotape.

Signed on behalf of landlord,   Jerry Underpin

Signed on behalf of lessees,   Ursula Plum

Deposit

Whether you are renting accommodation through the university or through the private rented sector, you will almost certainly be required to pay a deposit (usually equivalent to one month's rent). On top of one month's rent in advance, this can make quite a dent in your finances at the beginning of the academic year (see 'Budgeting', page 46).

The deposit is a bond to cover any damage or breakages that might occur during your tenancy. If you are renting from the university, they tend to be very even-handed – private landlords can be very different and many disputes arise over the withholding of deposits at the end of a lease. The NUS recommends that if you have a problem, you should talk to them – it may be possible to resolve the situation in the Small Claims Court. On no account should you withhold rent, as this puts you on the wrong side of the law.

References

You must have some written references – both personal and from a bank. You will need the following:

- proof of who you are (a letter from your GP, vicar or similar)

- proof that you are a student

- a personal character reference from a tutor or previous landlord

- bank statements

- copy of your grant or student loan agreement (to show that you can afford the rent).

The 1996 Housing Act

As a new tenant in the private rented sector, you will have almost no security. When you enter into an agreement to rent a property you will automatically be given an 'Assured Shorthold'. This means that you only have security of the property for six months.

If you feel insecure about this (it would be very inconvenient to be evicted two weeks before your exams) you could request that your landlord grant you an 'Assured Tenancy', which would give you security for twelve months. However, you may then end up responsible for the rent over the long summer vacation, which may not suit you.

Whilst there are some unpleasant lessors out there, many are understanding of students' needs and do make allowances for you. Treat them and their property well and they should reciprocate.

Statement of Terms

Ask your landlord for a written 'Statement of Terms'. They are legally obliged to supply one within 28 days. A 'Statement of Terms' is a document stating when the tenancy began, the amount of rent, when the rent is due, the length of the contract and when the rent is to be reviewed. The advantage of this document is that it protects both you and the landlord from any future misunderstandings about any of these details in the case of any dispute.

What Does Your Rent Cover?

In halls of residence the rent normally includes any charges for gas and electricity. In student flats these charges are often your responsibility.

Utilities

Before moving into your rented accommodation, telephone the local service providers, inform them of the exact date when your occupancy will begin and arrange for all the meters to be read. This will avoid any confusion over any arrears that might be outstanding – you don't want to be saddled with anyone else's bills. You may also need to pay a deposit. Services that you will be using include electricity, gas, telephone and water.

Council Tax

Council tax is a charge on both people and property, but the bill is sent to the property. As a student in full time education your liability to pay may be complicated by both where and with whom you live.

The first thing you must do is obtain a certificate from your institution to prove that you are a full time student – everyone living in the property needs one of these.

Exemptions

Only properties and not people can be made exempt from council tax under the current legislation. There are three types of dwelling for students that qualify as exempt:

1. **Halls of Residence**.

   Dwellings comprising student halls of residence, which can include self catering accommodation, are exempt from the council tax if they are provided predominantly for the accommodation of students. (The Minister for Further and Higher Education, 1993)

2. **Dwellings Occupied by Students**. Any house or flat where every adult is a full time student is exempt. This applies during the term time and vacations.

3. **Dwellings Left Empty by Students**. These are dwellings left empty where the owner (who has a freehold, leasehold or tenancy of at least six months) is a student. The owner must be a full time student within six weeks of leaving the dwelling empty.

   New legislation is being compiled to try to ensure that students in higher education may be exempted, but as the law stands at the moment, if council tax is owed on a property in which you are living, you may be jointly, and severally, liable.

   Me and my flatmates forgot to collect our certificates for the council tax. We ignored the demands for council tax and now they want to take us to court for arrears.

Running Repairs

Check with your landlord that he will take full responsibility for essential repairs, such as when the boiler croaks in the middle of winter or the roof gets sucked off by a tornado. Under your tenancy agreement, the landlord or landlady is almost certainly obliged to keep the following in good repair and good working order:

▦ the structure and exterior of your house, including drains and gutters

▦ the inside installations for the supply of water, gas, electricity and sanitation

▦ the installations for room heating and water heating.

In order to do this the landlord has a right of entry after reasonable notice (usually 24 hours, except in an emergency).

You could get the repairs done yourself and deduct the cost from your rent, but you should seek advice before you do this.

What To Do if You Have Problems with Your Accommodation

Here are some of the most common problems associated with student accommodation.

You Are Not Happy and Want To Move Out of Your Hall of Residence

Talk to the warden first of all. He or she may be able to resolve your problem so that you don't need to move. Remember that you are liable for the rent for the whole academic year, so someone else will need to take your place – preferably before you move. This may take a little time but shouldn't be a problem as halls of residence are popular.

Someone Has Dropped Out and You Are Saddled with Their Rent

When signing a lease, try to ensure that everyone takes equal responsibility. Advertise the vacancy all around the university and try to find a replacement as quickly as possible. If this is not possible, you might need to pass on details of the person who has dropped out to the landlord and ask them to pursue the matter themselves.

Your Landlord Is a Pig

If you are having problems with your landlord – not carrying out repairs, hassling you for rent, paying unexpected visits – speak to your Students' Union welfare officer. They may be able to have a word with the landlord. (They could, for instance, threaten to strike him off the University-approved register – such as Unipol at the University of Leeds). If the property has become unfit for occupation, you can get in touch with the Environmental Health Officer at the local council. They can force the landlord to carry out the repairs or, failing that, organize the repairs themselves and charge the landlord.

You Can't Get the Phone Connected Because of an Outstanding Bill

We rented this great house and when we moved in and paid our deposit and our rent we found we couldn't get the phone connected. The landlord owed them more than 100 quid and he'd gone to Peru.

If the landlord has an agent representing him, you should speak to the agent first about the problem. They may be able to sort it out, or they may suggest that you pay the bill and deduct it from the next month's rent. (Don't do this without getting a written confirmation from the agent.) Alternatively, talk to the customer services at the telephone company. Let them know that you are a new customer and unconnected to the landlord. They may accept you or ask you to pay a deposit against future bills.

Who To Contact with Problems

▦ Students' Union Welfare Officer

▦ College Accommodation Officer

▦ Housing Advice Centre

▦ Citizens' Advice Bureau

▦ Local Environmental Health Officer

▦ Health and Safety Executive's Gas Safety Action Line: 0800 300 363

2 *Getting There and Freshers' Week*

Getting Packed and Getting There

I must have a triple plug adaptor – that's what everyone says...

You've got somewhere to live. Now you have to pack up your life for the next year, or at least the next term. It's not like going on holiday – because you have to create your own home with everything you need and be self-reliant.

One of the biggest problems with university digs is the lack of space.

The first thing to decide on is how you are going to travel. A lot of students will be driven by their parents. It's nothing to be embarrassed about and has the advantages that you can load up the car, it's free, and you can give them back stuff that you find you don't need. Some students drive themselves but many have to rely on public transport. See Chapter 9 on the problems of having a car at university. Using public transport poses the most problems with regard to luggage.

Public transport

Remember you most probably do not have a student card yet. This will make a lot of difference to the cost in the future.

Coach

This is the cheapest form of travel – and the slowest. There may be luggage restrictions and you almost certainly won't be able to take a bike. If it's a long journey, take some grub – you do not want to start burning up your grant at the stops on the road.

Rail

You can get special fares (Apex and Super Apex), but they must be booked in advance and there will be some restrictions on which trains you can take. Make contact with your local railway station well in advance and find out what's on offer. You may have to change trains, so you don't want to be too overloaded, and you want to make sure that you leave yourself plenty of time to make the connection. If you reckon that you are going to be using rail transport frequently, you will be able to save money by obtaining a young persons' or student railcard.

Air

Going by air can be just as cheap as rail, especially if you are travelling to the opposite end of the country. Again, there are some very good special deals, but they also have to be booked well in advance – and remember to add on the cost of transport to and from the airport. Also, the luggage restrictions can be quite strict.

Arriving

When you arrive in your university town, you'll probably need to get a taxi to help you with all your stuff. Later on when you know your way around you will be able to manage with the local transport system.

What Should You Take and How Should You Take It?

The first time you go up to university, you will probably find that you have too many things to take personally, unless you go by car.

So it might be a good idea to pack some things in a box or trunk to be sent on ahead or just after you have settled in. Look through the Yellow Pages for local shippers and removal companies. With luck you should be able to arrange to send what you need as part of a bigger shipment – this works out much cheaper. Make sure that your goods are covered by the company's insurance or, better still, that the company is a member of the Guild of Removers and Storers. If you are going to do this you should bear in mind that things might be delayed – so what you send shouldn't be things you need immediately.

Whether you will be living in your own room in halls of residence, or sharing a university flat, there will be the same problem – lack of space. So, apart from being very careful to chose the right things to take with you, it is also vital to realize that once you get them there you will have to put them somewhere. Give yourself plenty of time to pack– don't leave it until just before you set off. Note: If you are living in halls of residence you will have to take everything home at the end of each term, as the rooms are used during the holidays for functions held by the university. This even includes posters on the wall.

Essential items (wherever you will be living)

Documents

▓ exam certificates

▓ college acceptance forms

▓ course reading lists

▓ grant forms and any correspondence on grant allocation

▓ National Insurance details

▓ passport

▓ birth certificate

▌ National Health registration card

▌ driving licence

▌ personal insurance certificate

▌ savings book

▌ phonecard

▌ credit cards

▌ travel tickets

▌ address book

▌ cheque-book

▌ several sets of passport photos (see 'Fresher's Week', page 34)

▌ accommodation documents, including contract.

> Have a separate box file to keep everything in.

Things to carry with you

▌ clothes

▌ one set of linen: sheets or duvet and duvet-cover, pillowcase and towel. (Some halls of residence may provide linen and towels, but they should let you know in advance if this is the case)

▌ toiletries and make-up

▌ medical kit

- sports' gear

- camera

- music system and favourite music

- corkscrew

- a starter pack of basic food items from home (see page 138)

- alarm clock

- photographs, etc.

Home-building gear (which can be sent separately, if necessary)

- mirror

- bedside lamp (essential)

- reading lamp

- bedside table (maybe)

- posters

- pictures

- wall-hangings

- the essential adaptor plug

- extension leads

- lampshade

- rug

- bedspread

- cushions

- waste-paper basket

- laundry bag

- floor cushion

- small table

- pin-board

- ashtrays

- kitchen equipment (see page 135)

- bluetack

- bike

- old A-level course notes (if relevant)

- slippers – (the kitchen floor can get really nasty)

- warm clothes: cosy jumper, gloves, warm boots and good coat

- plants

- hot-water bottle

- spare liver (for Freshers' Week)

- computer

- TV (see 'TV licence', page 47)

- boyfriend/girlfriend

- umbrella

▓ extra bed linen

▓ towels (including a separate towel for swimming)

▓ electric blanket

▓ book-ends

▓ spare light-bulbs and fuses

▓ washing powder

▓ indoor clothes drier to hang over radiator, or line for bathroom

▓ swimming costume

▓ tea towels (see 'Kitchen equipment', page 135)

▓ bog brush

▓ toilet cleaner

▓ screwdriver

▓ student tool kit (see page 63)

▓ student pharmacopeia (see page 87)

▓ student cooking kit (see page 138)

Essential items for studying

▓ folders

▓ stationery: pens, paper, etc

▓ post-its

▓ small tape-recorder for lectures

- box files

- dictionary

- reference books

- liquid paper

- hole punch

Things that you don't need (according to various students asked)

- tin of sardines

- wet suit

- four crap novels

- badminton racket

- parental worry

- map of France

- knee brace

- a girlfriend overseas

- six ties

- Spanish dictionary (when taking sciences).

It's a good idea to take some time to unpack. Try to make your space comfortable to begin with, even if it becomes a pigsty within a few days.

Storage

You are going to have no room in your room and so you may have to be creative with your storage. You could imagine that you are living in a much larger room but this won't solve your space problems.

You could use your packing containers for storage and furniture. If you use plastic storage boxes, get them in diminishing sizes so they can be packed inside each other and stored like Russian dolls. You can do that with suitcases as well. The good thing about using different-sized boxes is that they can be used for different things. A dozen plastic bin bags will always come in useful: for laundry, rubbish, fancy dress, as a raincoat or as ski-pants (two bags).

Here are a few other ideas that might be useful.

▌ A tea chest could double up as a bedside table.

▌ A plastic storage box can be used to keep dried food.

▌ Hang a laundry bag on back of wardrobe door for storage.

▌ Bring your tapes and CDs in their own storage box.

▌ Have a weatherproof bag to hang out of the window with your smelly trainers. You could put them on the window-sill, but they might get mouldy.

Freshers' Week

This is university – why, it's just one long party.

You have arrived, found your accommodation and unpacked. Now you are confronted by Freshers' Week. This is designed and organized by the students and the Union to help you to get acquainted with your fellow freshers and find out what is on offer outside lectures. There tend to be numerous opportunities to consume free or highly subsidized booze, and plenty of late nights, hangovers and disrupted eating patterns result in the condition of 'freshlag'. It may take you several weeks to recover but it is important to become involved. You may meet loads of people that you end up avoiding for the rest of your student days, but it is quite difficult, after this mad week, to meet and join people who have already started to form cliques. Apart from the reputation for the parties there are also opportunities to discover other things about your university.

Freshers' Fair

This is a showcase for the various societies, sports' clubs and groups that operate at your university. The event is usually sponsored by local businesses who will be trying to bribe you into becoming a patron of their wares by handing out freebies and discounts. Take a day-pack to collect any goodies and for any bumph that you might pick up from the societies and clubs.

Have a good look round before you start signing up for anything. Most clubs will have a subscription, so you should find out what they are offering, how much of your precious funds they want and how they spend your money. Always make sure they are recognized by your Students' Union.

It is a good idea to sign up for a couple of extra-curricular activities. You will have a chance to mix with students outside your course and from different years, rather than your flatmates. It can also be a useful addition to your CV (see chapter 10).

If you are interested in sport it is important to make contact with the club during Freshers' Week. Many of the trials for the teams are held either during the week or soon after and it may be difficult to be considered at a later stage. British universities are strong in a wide variety of sports, and even if you want to take only a recreational interest you will never have a better opportunity for advice, facilities and coaching.

Likewise, if amateur dramatics, orchestra or choir are your forté, now is the time to find out what performances are planned and when the auditions are.

There will be many societies after your subscriptions, from astronomy to zither-playing. Don't be tempted to join too many immediately. You will also need to assess how much spare time you are going to have. The armed services may also be represented – they may have an Officer Training Corps or an Air Squadron (see Chapter 3).

Be a little wary of evangelical and zealous religious societies – they sometimes have a reputation for being annoyingly persistent. However, many of the more mainstream religious societies can offer tremendous support for practising students. Universities can be targeted by cults who prey on the vulnerable. They may take control of your will as well as your finances. If you find yourself indoctrinated, be willing to discuss and listen to people who are not involved in the cult. Talk to the counsellor at the Students' Union.

Freshers' Ball

This is an informal party arranged for the Freshers and is the most important social event of the week. There is plenty of low cost grog, loud music and a late bar – this is probably where the onset of 'freshlag' begins.

It's a great event if you like that sort of thing. Everyone will be relaxed and it gives you a chance to meet your contemporaries. If you're not such a party animal, it is still worthwhile going along for a bit, just to get a feel for the community in which you are involved.

Departmental or Faculty Bash

This is rather more formal than the Freshers' Ball. You'll probably be offered a couple of glasses of Moroccan claret and a sausage roll. The bash gives you the opportunity to link up with fellow students on your course as well as to meet tutors and lecturers.

It will also help you to discover the ins and outs of the building in which you will be studying. You can get hold of information about your course; lecture, tutorial and seminar schedules; and reading lists. You can also find out what assignments you will be required to carry out. Whilst you are there you might as well sign on to your course – it's something you have to do anyway.

The departmental secretary is a jewel if you have any queries or need to get any information. He or she will know where to get hold of information, equipment, books and lecture notes – it is well worth cultivating a good working relationship.

The Modules Fair

I wish I'd gone along to the Modules Fair – I ended up being dumped into an economics course which was desperate.

Many degree courses, particularly non-sciences, are made up of compulsory modules and elective modules.

You can decide which elective modules you choose, although your director of studies may recommend ones related to your course. At the Modules Fair you will be able to find out what is available. The more interesting courses get filled up quickly, so the earlier you get there, the more choice you will have.

Other Events

There will be a host of other events organized for your entertainment, pleasure and initiation into student life: pub crawls, film festivals, concerts, cheap eats, clubbing, revues, quizzes.

You should receive an information pack of what's happening when you arrive. If not, get in touch with the Students' Union and also speak to other freshers. Have fun! No-one expects you to do anything academic during Freshers' Week.

Getting a Job To Top Up Your Finances

If you have decided that your finances are going to be stretched and want to get a part-time job, Freshers' Week is the time to start looking. The Students' Union will try to provide a variety of jobs for their members who need work to subsidize their costs, but you need to be on the ball to get one. Check out the notice-boards around the campus and at the Union and apply quickly. Amongst the jobs that may be available are helping in the Union bars and cafés, working in the libraries, for the University newspaper or radio station, and organizing entertainments such as concerts or films – whatever the job, the Union is the place to start looking.

Alternatively you may be able to find a part-time job in the town, working in a bar or a restaurant. Many advertise on their windows when they need staff. Or you could check out the local press and notice-boards in the town. When applying for a job. it is important to be polite and presentable (see Chapter 10).

Don't take on too much part-time work; leave enough time for your course requirements and also some time to enjoy being a student.

Boring Things That You Should Do in Freshers' Week

▓ Sort out your grant (if any).

▓ Sort out your student loan.

▓ Get your Union card (in Scotland, it is called Matriculation).

▓ Join the library.

▓ Register with a GP and dentist.

▓ Find your way around, public transport, etc.

▓ Sort out your timetable and choose courses.

▓ Buy some liver salts.

3 Money Matters

I can't afford to go to the pub until my grant cheque comes through...

You are now an almost fully independent adult, ensconced in your new digs. It may seem like the world is your oyster, but one of the downsides to your new independence is that you are now responsible for your finances and, as everyone knows, students subsist somewhere below the poverty line. To make matters worse, since the Dearing Report, students entering higher education are required to undertake greater financial burdens. Maintenance grants are being phased out and tuition fees are being brought in. To cope with these you are expected to take out loans. The NUS estimates that the 1998 intake of students will graduate with debts in excess of £10,000.

Maintenance Grants

Students starting in 1998 will get some help with maintenance in the form of a grant (for one year only). This is assessed on parental or spousal income and will be paid by your Local Education Authority (LEA). It will only apply for your first year. The balance of your requirements is to be made up in the form of student loans. For the academic year commencing 1999, all support for maintenance will be in the form of student loans.

How Do I Access My Maintenance Grant? (1998 Only)

You need to fill out an application form for a mandatory award from your LEA. Contact them and they will send you one, or you can collect a grant form from your school. You can apply as soon as you receive a conditional offer, except in Scotland, where you should only apply after you have been offered an unconditional place.

You will need to offer some proof of your parental or spousal income, either through wage slips or tax assessments. Ensure that your family contact their accountant (if they have one) in plenty of time.

When your application has been processed and if you are eligible, the LEA will send your grant cheque directly to the university or college. This is often delayed, so make sure that you have enough money to survive at the beginning of each term.

Student Loans

How Do I Take Out a Loan?

When you need to take out a loan, contact your university or college Loans Administrator. You can get details about this from your university or college Students' Union. You will be given an eligibility questionnaire to fill in. This ascertains whether you meet the criteria and how much you can borrow. You must have with you:

▓ birth or adoption certificate

▓ mandatory award letter

▓ evidence of your bank or building society account number.

If you qualify, your university or college will pass your details on to the Student Loans Company, who will pay the loan directly into your account.

You can stage the payments over the three terms – a good idea if you want to avoid running out of funds after one and a half terms. You can only make one application per year. Calculate your finances carefully and make sure that you borrow enough.

Repayment of Student Loans

This is not something that you need to worry about for a few years. Once you have graduated and start earning, you will have to start making repayments – but only if you are earning enough money. From 1998, loans for new entrants will be repaid, via the Inland Revenue, based on 9 per cent of gross income above £10, 000. The amount of time it takes to repay the loan will also depend on your income and the size of the loan. The loans are index-linked to the rate of inflation from when you take them out. They are about the cheapest money that you can borrow. Table 3.1 shows the estimates for weekly repayments against your future salary under current government policy.

Table 3.1: Student loan repayments (Source: DFEE, January 1998)

Annual income (£)	Monthly repayment (£)
10,000	0
12,000	15
15,000	37
17,000	52
20,000	75

Whizz kids borrow and invest in high-interest accounts – very risky.

Tuition Fees

The families of younger students beginning their degrees in 1998 or after will be expected to make a contribution of up to £1,000 towards the costs of tuition. This contribution is instead of the previous contribution towards maintenance and is reckoned to be an equitable burden.

The size of the contribution is to be assessed on parental or spousal income. If the gross income is less than £23,000 no fees will have to be paid. Only when the income exceeds £35,000 will the full £1,000 be payable.

Note: gap-year students starting in 1998, whose university place had been confirmed by 1 August 1997, will be treated in the same way as students who began their higher-education course in 1997.

Mandatory Awards

Every student who is a British citizen or a citizen of an EU country who has been ordinarily resident in the UK for at least the previous three years is eligible for a mandatory award. This pays the balance of the tuition fees after the parental or spousal contribution. When you submit your application for a grant you will receive a notice from your LEA confirming this.

Other Forms of Finance

Scholarship

With the advent of tuition fees some universities may offer scholarships to help with the cost of tuition fees. For example, the University of Wales is offering eight scholarships of £1,000 in various subjects from English to Engineering. The scholarships are awarded by competition through an essay, project or assignment. Contact the admissions office of the institute you wish to attend if you need information about these kind of scholarships.

Some charities offer scholarships. They are usually in a specific subject at a particular institute. For example, there is a scholarship at Glasgow University for geography. You should be able to find information about these from your school's careers office.

Sponsorship

Some major companies offer sponsorship to students. These sponsorships tend to be aimed at the sciences, although it may be possible to obtain one if you are studying a language. The arts tend to be under-represented.

One of the advantages of getting sponsored is that the companies often provide employment during the long summer vacation.

Sandwich Course (Not How To Make Interesting Triple-decker BLT's!)

A sandwich course includes an industrial year in the middle for which you will be paid. It is up to you, with the help of your institution, to find a suitable placement. In return the company you work for may help with the expenses of your education and may also offer you a full-time job after you have completed your degree.

Army Cadetship/Bursary

If you decide before or early in your degree that you want to pursue a career in the Army, then you may be able to qualify for a cadetship. If you pass the selection procedure, you attend a short course at Sandhurst in the long vacation. The Army will pay you during your time at university and the Ministry of Defence will pay for your tuition. On completion of your degree (provided it is academically good enough) you will return for a commissioning course to Sandhurst, before spending a minimum of five years in the armed services. During your time at university you must carry out training with the university Officer Training Corps and also spend at least one month of the long vacation attached to regular unit.

If you feel that you only wish to commit yourself to three years in the services, then you could qualify for an Army Undergraduate Bursary. You will be given some financial support, as well as opportunities to undertake paid training. This will not affect your grant in any way, as it is exempt from assessment or income tax. When you graduate you attend a commissioning course at Sandhurst, before serving a minimum of three years.

If you change your mind and do not wish to serve the required time in the army, you will have to refund all monies paid out for a cadetship or bursary.

It is also possible to get sponsorship from the Royal Navy and the Royal Air Force.

Discretionary Grants

Local Education Authorities offer a limited number of special grants for students who do not qualify for a mandatory grant (for example, if you have already done a degree). The authority decides to whom and for how much the grant is awarded. You should make an early application for these. The award could be equivalent to a mandatory award and be paid on the same terms. Discretionary grants are not available in Scotland.

Access Funds

Each university or college is given a fund by the government to help out students in severe financial hardship. Money from these access funds is not easy to obtain. You usually have to prove that you have explored every possible avenue of financial support before you will even be considered for an access fund award.

Disabled Students' Allowance

If your disability means that you incur additional expenses on your course you may qualify for an additional allowance. This might pay for special equipment, readers, helpers and extra travel costs. Any equipment you buy becomes your property and you may donate it to your college or university on graduation if you no longer need it. Disabled students' allowances are paid as part of the mandatory award; they will not be means tested from 1998/9.

Bank Overdraft

Having a bank overdraft is almost a prerequisite of being a student. Most banks offer very tempting interest-free overdraft facilities, hoping to win your loyalty for life. But you should try to use an overdraft as a final resort. Don't forget that next term's maintenance cheque or loan may be delayed – and then you really would need the overdraft.

Note – an overdraft has to be arranged with the bank before you can use the facility (see below, 'Your bank account').

Loans and Credit Cards

The NUS strongly recommend that you do not get yourself heavily committed to finance companies or interest-free loans offered by stores. You will almost certainly find that the monthly repayments are beyond your budget, the interest will start piling up and the next thing you know you'll be up shit creek without a paddle.

Likewise credit cards should be avoided unless you are a highly disciplined individual. But they are useful as a last resort, emergency backup – for if you suddenly need to travel to a sick relative, or something like that – not to replace your bust hi-fi or buy a motorbike or ball-gown.

Part-time Work

Student unions try to provide opportunities for paid work in their various facilities to help out their members (see Chapter two). You should check out what is available and do this as soon as you reach university for the first time. Competition is fierce. Work could be in a bar or café, library, on the student newspaper, or on the radio – there are all sorts of things. Or you could get a part time job in the town in a shop or pub. Look in the local press for opportunities, and do not over-commit yourself. Research has shown that students who work more than 15 hours per week drop one grade in their degree classification.

Getting Into Debt

As students are so poor they are very vulnerable to debt. Debt in itself is not a problem, so long as you can keep up the necessary repayments. By the time you graduate you will probably have accrued various sorts of debt.

As already mentioned, you will be in debt to the government for your student loan. This is out of your hands, so you don't need to worry too much about this – you can look upon it as a tax for something you have already had.

Then you will probably have built up an overdraft with your

bank which they will expect you to start paying off. They may start charging you interest.

If you find you have mismanaged your finances badly, your credit card is to the limit, your rent is due, the electricity bill and the phone bill have just arrived and you have overshot your overdraft limit – then you are in trouble. As soon as you realize you are in trouble you need to sit down and sort out all the money that you owe, work out what needs paying urgently and draw up some sort of plan how to deal with this. The Students' Union should have a debt counsellor who can offer you good advice. The counsellor will help you to draw up the strategy, and you may then be able to approach your bank and obtain a temporary increase for your overdraft facility. Or the counsellor will show you how to deal with your creditors so that they remain reasonably happy with you.

It is vital that once you have got into a financial pickle that you adhere to any strategy that you have proposed.

Destroy your credit and account cards, budget very carefully, do not overspend and try not to get too depressed. Debt can have a serious effect on both your mental and physical health.

Budgeting

To avoid letting your finances get out of control, you should make a termly budget of what you think you are going to need to spend, what money you are going to have and how much you might have left over for yourself. Try to think of everything. To begin with you will probably be horribly wrong, but as you go on you will become wiser about your spending patterns.

Table 3.2 shows a typical budget for a fresher. The first column shows the income and outgoings that the fresher budgeted for; the second column shows what really happened. In the outgoings, the student overlooked the £100 deposit on the room, and also had a wild time in Freshers' Week – which turned out to be more like three weeks. As a result of this, not much in the way of books or toiletries were bought, and the student hung on without doing any laundry for the last four weeks, so that Mum could do it in the vacation. With this experience next term's budget should be easier – but it is impossible to foresee everything. You could add in a ten per cent contingency fund to cover surprise items. And try to avoid grant euphoria. Suddenly having a four-figure bank account does not mean you're rich – you might just survive the term.

Table 3.2: Termly budget (all figures in pounds)

	Virtual	Reality
Maintenance grant/family/loan	1150	1150
Part-time work	150	180
Miscellaneous (holiday earnings, gifts etc)	320	420
Total	1620	1750
Outgoings		
Accommodation	630	730
Telephone	30	50
TV license and rental	67	67
Food	120	260
Insurance	12	12
Transport	40	52
Books/stationery	120	42
Club fees	15	15
Clothing	100	45
Toiletries	32	16
Laundry	25	10
Entertainment	200	460
Cigarettes	100	150
Total	1491	1909
Balance	+129	-159

Your Bank Account

Choosing a Bank

You must have a bank or building society account that accepts direct credits in order to be eligible for a student loan. All the main high-street banks compete vigorously for your account and offer freebies to tempt you. Here are some things to consider when you are deciding which one to go for.

▓ Is the branch conveniently located?

▓ Does it have a student adviser?

▓ Does it offer an interest-free overdraft?

▓ Does it give you a cheque-book and guarantee card?

▓ Does it have a good network of cash machines?

▓ Will it pay you monthly interest?

▓ Does it send you monthly statements?

▓ Can you apply for a fee-free credit card?

▓ What freebies are on offer?

To open a student account you will need to prove your identity and give details of your course. If you already have a bank account at home, tell them that you are becoming a student and ask them to open a student account for you and to transfer the account to the branch nearest the campus – and don't forget to ask for your freebies.

Running a Bank Account

It is very useful to have some idea about your financial state of affairs at all times. Always make sure you fill in your cheque-book stubs and paying-in book assiduously.

Always ask for a receipt when withdrawing money from a cash machine. Most cheque-books have a space for you to keep a running balance; keep this up-to-date and then, if you lose track, it is easy to request a balance from a machine. (But be aware that some cheques might not have cleared.)

Check your bank statements against your stubs. Occasionally banks do make mistakes; if one occurs, you should notify your bank immediately. Keep in touch, respond to letters and, if you expect that you might need to exceed your overdraft, contact the bank in advance and make arrangements. It is very expensive for you if the bank starts writing to you.

Finally, look after your bank documents and cards. Don't keep your cheque-book and cheque card together. Memorize and destroy your pin number. If you cannot remember it, then make sure your notes of what it is is nowhere near your cashcard. If you lose anything, contact your bank immediately so that they can stop any transactions.

Saving Tips for Your Budget

■ Fill yourself up on foods like pasta or rice before going out in the evening. You won't get so drunk, you won't be able to drink as many pints and that irresistible, greasy Chinese takeaway may not seem quite so attractive.

■ Go to the supermarket late in the day and look for special bargains. Items that are near to their sell-by date are marked down but you need to eat them straight away.

■ Make your own picnic lunch.

■ Try to eat regular meals and avoid expensive snacking.

■ Persuade your parents to stock you up with basics at the beginning of each term.

▓ Marry a millionaire.

▓ Get a part-time job in a restaurant – free food.

▓ Get a part-time job in a pub, while you work you can't be spending money on the other side of the bar.

▓ Club together with your flatmates and cook meals for a group.

▓ Avoid pre-prepared foods. Half the money you pay is for the packaging.

▓ Check local markets and buy veggies and fruit in season.

▓ If you are in halls of residence, eat the meals that you've already paid for.

▓ Eat in the university or Students' Union cafés – they are subsidized and cheap.

▓ Find a boyfriend or girlfriend who is a gourmet cook and needs somebody to appreciate and praise their efforts.

▓ Take all the clothes you need when you go up to university – including the embarrassing woollie your grandma knitted last Christmas. It might become a fashion statement.

▓ Look for bargains in charity shops, jumble sales, flea markets and car-boot sales.

▓ Cut down on your heating by dressing warmly, and avoid getting too cold. (The secret is to keep your feet, hands and head warm.)

▓ Don't heat your house at night. Make sure you have enough warm bedclothes.

▓ Wear warm jumpers and socks when you are studying in the winter. Jump around like a crazed orang utan every now and then to get your blood circulating.

- Keep an eye on notice-boards, websites and the press for second-hand deals on things like books, bikes, etc.

- Sell any stuff that you don't need (as long as it is yours).

- Give up smoking.

- Give up drinking.

- Give up being a student and become chief executive of a multinational corporation.

4 *Living Skills*

Who's eaten my last slice of bread?

Until you go to university, you will probably have shared your life and education with people from a similar background to yourself. One of the greatest things about university is the diversity of people that you will be meeting and mixing with: people from all over the country and from all over the world, people of different religions, people from various ethnic backgrounds, disabled people and mature students, gay people – even people of the opposite sex may be a new experience for you, if you have had a single-sex education. Some people might have loads of dosh whilst others are unbelievably skint.

Keep an open mind and try not to fall into the trap of stereotyping people. Remember that you are all undergraduates at the same university and are all probably confronted by very similar problems. People are much deeper than any single category in which you might classify them.

In a way, university is a sort of microcosm of the world – albeit one made up of people who have achieved academic success to progress into higher education. Look upon it as a chance to learn about and enjoy life beyond the narrow horizons of your street at home.

As a fresher, you are more than likely to be allocated your first accommodation. You won't have a choice as to whom you will be living in close proximity with. The accommodation office does try to put together people with similar backgrounds, but generally they don't make a very good job of it.

It can be very nerve-wracking sitting on your humble pile of possessions in your new flat awaiting the arrival of your new flatmates. It will be the same for them.

I arrived on Saturday. My roommate came on Sunday and I was dreading it. I thought she was going to be some Gothic lesbian – that was my worst nightmare – but she turned out more conservative than me. We got on really well.

When your flatmates have all arrived, you will all have a chance to get in some practice for your standard Freshers' Week conversation. Introduce yourself to Henry and Fiona and over the first cup of coffee or bottle of wine you will discover:

▧   what course Henry is studying

▧   a yawningly interesting account of Fiona's gap year

▧   where Fiona lives

▧   that Henry is a fanatical philatelist

▧   and several more boring things.

At this stage you shouldn't form any hard and fast judgements. Henry may seem to be the world's greatest crashing bore and Fiona may be overwhelmingly self-assured, but in reality – and just like you – they are terribly nervous and just dealing with a lack of confidence by putting up a front. Anyway, you have got nine months to come to a conclusion as to how you feel about them, and you might develop an interest in stamp-collecting.

Business Meeting

If you are living in a flat it is important to get everyone together as soon as possible and discuss how you are going to coexist. It is best to do this at an early stage, before people's habits start causing rifts.

Draw up a draft document of intentions which could be reviewed after a few weeks.

Points To Discuss At Your First Meeting

Using the phone Should you use a charge card only or rely on people's honesty to write down all the calls they make? Who is responsible for the bill?

Security It is important to lock up and keep windows closed, especially in the summer when the house is empty.

Other bills and responsibility It is a good idea to share the responsibility of bills, so that each person is responsible for something, rather than one person being responsible for everything.

Noise pollution Discuss being quiet late at night and what to do about noisy friends staying.

Food Are you going to have a food kitty for food that you are all going to share? You should each have your own cupboard and shelf. It is cheaper to cook for several people, so perhaps you should decide to have a communal meal a couple of times a week.

Washing-up This is always a major problem. Do you wash up as you go or wait until there is nothing except the carpet to eat off? Perhaps you can decide on a weekly rota for washing-up and clearing up the kitchen. It may be better to do it in pairs.

Bathroom How long you can stay in the bath if someone else needs it? What are you going to do about rationing water – particularly hot water. How are you going to deal with keeping the loo clean – Mum's no longer round to deal with the skid-marks.

Smoking Yes or no? If yes, where?

This is a serious part of coexisting; but it should be approached in a reasonably light-hearted way. The intention of the meeting is to draw up some ground rules that you all understand. They'll probably have flown out of the window by week two, but it is worth trying for the sake of happy communal living.

You have all been thrown together by the caprice of some faceless accommodation officer.

> *OK, Jenny likes heavy metal and Sue is a Jazz fan but she smokes. They'll get on – smoking and heavy metal are one and the same thing.*

You don't all have to be the closest of friends but it does help if you can get on. Or at least try to get on.

Living together can put enormous strains on relationships and in many ways it is best not to share with your closest friends. If they live somewhere else, then at least you have somewhere to escape to when the pressures of your flat get on top of you. Idealists should not live in student flats – so don't expect to be blissfully happy.

However good your communal intentions are, your carefully planned strategy for a happy and efficient household will inevitably break down and there will be moments of petty bickering that can escalate into real bad feeling.

> *People on my corridor get sick of each other. There are a couple of people who get very homesick and come and cry on you when you're trying to write an essay. I had a falling out with my best friend, but that's just because we spent too much time together.*

Typical Problems and Some Solutions

Someone Never Cleans the Bath

Elect a keeper of the bath plug.

The Washing-up Is Never Done

Wash up as you go along or as you need, and have a rota for a weekly clean up.

Someone Is Hogging the Bath and All the Hot Water

Get into the bathroom earlier.

Bullying

This is not something that is confined to the school playground. It can occur in all walks of life, including at university. It is unlikely to manifest itself physically but more often appears in a form of mental harassment.

> *There was, however, also a nightmare flatmate. How can I forget the pleasurable moment when she licked her cold sores, complained about her verruca as she wandered barefoot around the kitchen and gave us unwanted tips on how to give our boyfriends a better wank. She became the victim of a lot of bitching. It was easy to go along with but we were totally out of order.*

You might all agree that you have the flatmate from hell and it is easier to close ranks and exclude that person. Resorting to bitching can easily become bullying. You have only to imagine yourself in that position to realize that it is untenable both for the victim and the aggressors. It is best to confront personal differences as early as possible. If this doesn't seem to have any effect, you need to find alternative ways of dealing with the problem. Trying to avoid the situations that annoy you may not always be possible but you should try to be patient and tolerant, and remember you probably have some habits that irritate other people as well.

If you find that you are a victim of bullying, one solution to the problem is to find somewhere else to live. This may seem a drastic solution. Alternatively, you might confront your tormentors individually. Tell them how bad they are making you feel. They may be acting unconsciously. Look at yourself and see if there are ways you could change to improve the situation. If it is unbearable, speak to the student welfare officer or the resident warden.

Racism and Prejudice

This is just an ignorant expression of fear because someone is different. Unfortunately it can become a big issue if it is promoted by some radical group, whether it be politically, religiously or morally motivated. If you are undergoing serious harassment because you belong to a marginalized group, you should inform the Students' Union immediately. Remember that you have exactly the same rights as anyone else at University.

Other Problems

I was put into this brilliant flat with three other girls. The first weekend, Rachel's boyfriend came to stay for the weekend. We all liked him, but then he came back again in the middle of term and ended up staying till the end of term. What really pissed us off was that he sat around all day smoking and drinking beer, using our coffee and stuff, and never offered to contribute.

A perennial student problem: other people's guests outstaying their welcome. You should try to reach an agreement beforehand about what the ground rules are – and stick to them. In this case, maybe you only allow house guests at the weekend. But stay a little flexible.

We had a real problem after a few weeks. It was obvious that Brian wasn't too up on personal hygiene. He'd worn the same clothes all term and basically he smelt. So one day we ran him a bath and all sat in the kitchen with clothes-pegs on our noses till he came back from lectures.

It is a good idea to face a dilemma like this head on but with a sense of humour. Brian might have been slightly hurt, but he was probably completely unaware how much he was hurting his flatmates' delicate olfactory organs.

In my second year, I decided to shack up with my girlfriend. We thought we'd save loads of money by sharing a room. As

> *it turned out, we constantly argued and I agreed to move out at Christmas. She got lumbered with the extra rent and I was homeless. We don't talk to each other now.*

Living with someone with whom you are romantically connected is a serious commitment and needs to be thought about very carefully. The strains of cohabiting can pull the relationship apart. Anyway, if it is strong enough, it will survive you both having your own space. Similar problems can also affect close friendships.

> *Every time I go to the fridge I find that some bastard has half-inched most of my grub.*

This is a very difficult problem. You all need to agree on what is common food and arrange a kitty to pay for it. You also need to agree that some space in the fridge is dedicated to each flatmate. Also, each flatmate should have their own shelf in the food cupboard. It's a good idea to label your spices and dry goods. If this doesn't work out, you may have to resort to keeping non-perishable goods in your room.

> *My flatmate kept borrowing my favourite summer dress. I wouldn't have minded if he'd asked; and anyway, he looked ridiculous.*

No judgement of personal tastes here, which is good, but again it is a tale of pilfering. Try to ensure that your room has a lock on it and keep your possessions safely secured inside. (The lock may be an essential requirement for any insurance cover that you buy.)

Doing Your Laundry

> *All my clothes have gone pink. What shall I do?*

Even the most committed of grungy students finally give in to washing their clothes – probably as a result of complaints from fellow students about the pong, or the fact that the clothes are now standing up by themselves and are even offering to take notes for their owner at lectures.

Some of you will never have had to wash a garment before in your life – the handy laundress or launderer (along with the cook, seamstress, cleaner, etc) does it for you. However, if you are not into monochrome clothes (pink, grey or sludge-coloured) then the following information might be of use to you.

If you live in a hall of residence or in a student flat, there will most likely be a laundry room – usually with three machines for about 40 students. Some use money, whilst others use tokens or a card which costs about £5 for three washes and three drys. It's not cheap.

The Laundry Room

The laundry room is usually outside the building, often in a cold room. If it is isolated you should team up with a friend and do your laundry together, as this is safer and more companionable. There is no TV or other entertainment – bring a book, a plastic bag or basket for dirty clothes and linen, washing-powder, conditioner and a drink. It usually takes about two hours. This can be boring, so sometimes you have to leave your stuff while it's in the machine and go back to your room. The only problem with doing that is that if someone else wants to use the machine and your cycle is finished, they often dump your clothes on the dirty floor. It's a good idea to take either a large plastic bag with your name on or a basket, which people can put your washing in.

The other drawback is that the machines might not be free. I guess all these things are one of the reasons why it's easier to let your clothes stay dirty.

Doing the Wash

Buy a box of washing-powder from the supermarket. It's much cheaper in the long run.

Most items of clothing have a label that gives instruction as to how to wash them. But, being a student, you probably won't be able to afford to separate your laundry into seven different categories. Be careful with new brightly coloured items bought as a bargain from the local market. The colour will almost certainly come out in the wash. Try them out by hand-washing first. As a general rule, put all your coloured things together and wash at a moderate temperature. Woollen items should be washed at quite a cool temperature on a delicate cycle. You can always wash them by hand. If you're posh enough to have cashmere or angora, then you can probably afford a laundry service. You will need to wash white linens and cottons at higher temperature – you can probably chuck your bed linen into this wash as well, as it should be colour-fast.

Drying

This is where the danger of shrinkage is greatest, especially with woollen articles. These should be dried naturally or at a very low temperature. Wrap the item in a towel and twist the towel around to squeeze out the excess water. (Your laundry partner can help you.) Then find somewhere in your room to spread the article out to dry in its own time.

It is much easier to iron clothes that are slightly damp. So, don't put your clothes in the drier for too long. If they are bone-dry they will probably be horribly creased as well. However, if you are not planning to iron them immediately, if at all, they may go mouldy. In this case, dry them completely. When the drier has finished, fold the clothes to avoid them becoming excessively crumpled.

Ironing

Use a water spray salvaged from some old bottle of cleaning liquid to dampen the clothes slightly (if you haven't got a steam iron.) All clothes should have a label that tells you at what temperature to set the iron. Here's a rough guide.

Table 4.1: Temperatures for ironing clothes

Hottest ***	Linen, cotton
Medium **	Wool
Low *	Silk
Very low	Nylon

Never leave the iron resting in one place when ironing, and never leave it turned on. Put it somewhere safe and out of the way to cool off.

Never iron directly on the carpet or work surface.
If you don't have an ironing-board, use a towel or blanket.

Ironing a shirt

1. Flatten out the sleeves so that the seam is at the bottom. Press the cuffs first, then the sleeve. Turn it over and press the other side of the sleeve. Repeat with the other sleeve.

2. Iron the collar and the panel of material at the top of the back. Do the collar both sides and don't try to iron in the crease – it should reform naturally. You can use spray starch, but I wouldn't bother.

3. Finally iron the body of the shirt, working your way around with a smooth action. If it has pockets, do these first.

4. Alternatively, just iron the collar a bit at the front and wear a V-necked sweater.

Ironing a pair of jeans (unlikely)

1. Lay the jeans out on the floor. Smooth them out with your hand, so that the inside seams are flat and on the inside edge of the legs. Make sure the pockets are pushed down and flat and do up the fly. At this stage you could fold the two legs together, and lay them under your mattress. (Don't forget they are there.)

2. Starting at the bottom of each leg, work the iron up to the top, pressing both sides of each leg.

3. Pull the top of the jeans over the ironing-board and press the seat and the front area.

On the other hand you may want to present yourself in that age-old student fashion statement, the crumpled look.

Useful Tips for Removing Stains

Fresh bread is a good stain remover – sometimes a slice of bread will remove make-up stains from clothes. It will also remove light marks on wallpaper. Try using it to clean up old photographs – but rub gently.

Beer

If you spill beer on washable fabrics, soak them in cold water immediately, then wash as usual. If you spill beer on the carpet, pour some soda water over it, or sponge with cold water and then shampoo it. Better still don't spill it, drink it.

Red wine

If you spill red wine on your clothes or the carpet, cover the patch immediately with generous quantities of salt. Leave it to draw out the wine and then wash as usual.

Other nastiness

If you find you have grease, oil, butter, vomit, poo, snot, old sweat marks or urine on your clothes, here's what you do. First of all, scrape off excess muck, then soak in nappy powder (sold in the supermarket in the baby section; it is used for nappies but can be used for all bodily fluids) or rub with stain-removing soap (also available in the supermarket) and then shove the clothes in the wash.

Grass stains (not that sort)

Rub the stained area with runny honey and leave for a while, before washing in the normal way.

Things That Need Tools

How many psychology students does it take to change a light bulb?
Just one – but the light-bulb has to want to change.

It is a good idea to have a few basic tools to hand, as there are one or two very minor repairs you can carry out yourself. If something electrical stops working, try a new fuse first of all. You might feel a bit stupid lugging your 50kg hi-fi to the repair shop only to find that the only problem was a blown fuse – that's if they tell you; they may charge you £50 to replace it. But, realistically, you don't need to be an expert at DIY to survive. Any major problems should be dealt with by the landlord or landlady.

Student Tool Kit

▓ flat screwdrivers, two sizes

▓ cross-head (Phillips) screwdriver

▓ medium-weight claw-hammer

▓ craft knife

▓ pair of pliers

▓ spare fuses, various sizes

▓ assortment of screws and nails

▓ duct tape.

Don't forget – if you start banging nails in the walls all round your room, you may lose your deposit at the end of the year.

How To Change a Plug

1. Clear a space on your table. Arrange the plug so that it rests without being tugged by the cable.

2. Turn the plug on its back and release the central screw that holds the two halves together.

3. Unscrew the two screws holding the cable in place where it enters the plug.

4. Unscrew the three small brass screws holding the wire strands in the terminal blocks.

5. Trim back the outside insulating sheath to expose the three internal wires. Be careful not to nick their insulation.

6. Turn the wires up and trim them to length, so that when they are fitted the cable clip presses down on the outside of the insulation sheath.

7. Rewire as follows. Green and yellow (earth) to top centre; blue (neutral) to left-hand side; and brown (live) to right-hand terminal with fuse.

8. Tighten cable clip and refix.

Tip: place any loose screws on a sheet of white paper so that they are easy to find.

Note: to change a fuse you just need to open the plug and lever out the old fuse before you replace it with a new one of the same amperage.

The Loo Won't Stop Flushing

A temporary repair can be affected by lifting up the cistern cover and wedging the bright plastic float as high as possible so that the water stops flowing – then call your landlord to get a plumber.

Changing the Barrel on a Cylinder Lock

You may want to do this, since you don't know who has got keys to the lock. A new barrel costs a few pounds – if you're splitting the cost with several others this is not too bad. Check the exact make of the lock that you are changing and be certain to buy a new cylinder that is compatible.

Take out the screws holding the body of the lock from the inside of the door. Then take out the screws holding the flat plate and the cylinder on the inside of the door. Remove the flat plate and the cyclinder. Push the barrel out through the front of the door. Take the barrel to a locksmith for an identical replacement. Ask the locksmith to cut the flat connecting bar that goes through the door to the same length as the original. Insert the new barrel and fix the plate back on to the door. Carefully realign the body, ensuring the connecting bar goes into the slot, and screw on to the door.

Changing a Mortice Lock

For the same reason as above, you may wish to change your mortice lock. Unscrew the face plate on the door and then unscrew the two screws holding the lock body. Lever the lock out of the door and take it to a locksmith. He will either replace the locking mechanism or replace the whole lock with another one the same size. Then simply replace the lock body in the door, screw it in and replace the face plate. It's dead simple dealing with dead locks.

Drawers Are Sticking (Buy Bigger Pants)

This sometimes happens and can be very irritating.

Take the drawer out of the chest of drawers. You should be able to see wear marks where it is sticking. Sandpaper these to a smooth surface and then rub on a thin layer of candle wax. Repeat this on the chest.

Broken Window

This may be a little advanced but glaziers are expensive.

Wear some gloves. Remove all the broken glass by tapping it out with a hammer. There will be some small pins (sprigs) holding the glass in position which you can pull out easily with a pair of pliers. Remove any old putty, so that the surface of the reveals (the part of the window frame in which the glass sits on the putty) is clean and smooth. Wrap the broken glass in newspaper before throwing it out.

Measure the size of the opening and have the new glass cut 3mm smaller in each dimension. Buy 1lb of putty. Get some new sprigs at the same time.

Spread a thin layer of bedding putty around the reveal, position the new glass and fix in position with the sprigs. Now apply putty to the outside of the glass so that it forms a 45-degree angle. Shape it with a knife dipped in water. Excess putty can be cleaned off with methylated spirit (do not drink this). After a few weeks the putty should be painted.

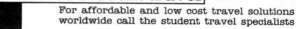

The Daily Telegraph Guides

Working For Yourself
Eighteenth Edition
Godfrey Golzon

This practical and straightforward guide offers advice on every aspect of starting up your own business. It includes advice on:

- legal requirements
- account and record-keeping
- self-assessed taxation and national insurance
- raising capital and getting paid
- accessing government training and advice

"Virtually the standard work on the subject. Highly recommended" THE GUARDIAN

£10.99 • Paperback • 07494 2677 2
256 pages • 1998

KOGAN PAGE, 120 Pentonville Road, London N1 9JN
Tel: 0171 278 0433 Fax: 0171 837 6348

5 *Study Skills*

Am I the only one out of 170 who doesn't understand the lecture?

Studying – and How To Manage It

Now that you are a university student, the amount of commitment you make to your studying is left pretty much up to you. There won't be teachers chasing you around to find out why you haven't been to lectures or where your essay is. It is not that they don't care – you may be summoned to your tutor or director of studies to explain your lack of production and ultimately thrown off the course. But you are considered to be an adult, capable of making your own decisions and organizing your own life.

> I would say from my vast experience of all these students, not to mention my daughter's experiences and my own as a student, that one of the most difficult transitions from the environment of school to the environment of higher education is in terms of independent study. (University professor)

Teaching Methods at University

There are a number of different ways in which knowledge is imparted to you.

Lectures

Lectures are often given to as many as 100 students at a time. The lecturer will present a talk, often using visual aids such as charts, overhead projections and samples. The lecturer may be a member of the teaching staff or a guest speaker. Some lecturers provide a précis of the subject matter. Occasionally time may be assigned for questions and answers. However, due to the size of the audience, there may be very little personal contact.

To make the most of your lectures, remember the following.

▌ Give yourself plenty of time to get to lectures, especially if you have to travel by public transport. If you arrive a few minutes late, firstly you will disturb your fellow students; secondly you will miss the beginning of the lecture in which its key aim may have been outlined; and finally, by the time you've settled down, half of the lecture will probably have passed.

▌ Make sure that you have everything you need for taking notes: paper, a good surface to write on, pen, any text required and possibly a tape-recorder. Your exams may well be based on your lectures.

The number of lectures that you have will depend on the course that you have chosen. They are generally not compulsory – but what's the point of being at university if you don't go to lectures? Also, keep an eye out for general lectures organized by the university or other departments that may be related to your course or of interest to you, as well as open lectures that other universities in the area may have.

If you have to miss a lecture, borrowing a fellow student's notes may not help. Their particular method of shorthand may be incomprehensible to you. See if you can obtain some notes from the lecturer. Or, if a précis is handed out, ask a fellow student to collect a copy for you. It is also useful and courteous to inform a lecturer in advance if you have to miss their talk. If you do this, the lecturer will be more inclined to arrange for you to have the information.

Tutorials

Tutorials are a personal way of teaching. You have them with a tutor, either on your own or with a couple of other students. How much you get out of a tutorial will depend on how much preparation you do beforehand and, of course, how you relate to the tutor.

> *At the first tutorial we had, the tutor refused to teach us because we hadn't done the reading.*

If you have a shared tutorial it may well be worth meeting the other students beforehand to draw up salient points that you all wish to discuss.

Seminars

At seminars, several students come together under the supervision of a tutor or lecturer to discuss a particular issue of the course. Seminars usually consist of a larger group than tutorials.

If seminars are part of your course, remember the following points.

▨   It is essential to prepare for seminars in advance so that you can bring up particular matters that seem important and relevant.

▨   It is quite normal to be asked to make a short presentation to your group for discussion during a seminar. Plan your talk carefully, make notes on postcards or index cards and practise several times beforehand – in front of your flatmates (poor souls, but they'll get you back when it's their turn!).

Field Work, Lab Work or Studio Work

Depending on your choice of course, you may be required to carry out projects and experiments in the field or a laboratory.

Field trips are usually scheduled for the vacations and many last a few weeks. You could be assigned to a partner or a team for this. Your accommodation (probably pretty basic) and your travel will most likely be subsidized.

You will need to perform experiments if you are studying a science. The presentation of your results and conclusions could form an important part of your final degree.

Likewise, for students of the fine arts, performing arts and architecture there will be studio time, sometimes supervised. It is very important, as the portfolio you build up will represent a large proportion of your final assessment.

As many of the above activities can take some time (and can go wrong) it is sensible to get down to them in plenty of time.

Sources and Resources

Books

Before you go up to university, you will probably be sent a book and reading list (we advise you to avoid rushing out to buy everything). There may be some texts that you are encouraged to read before you start. Try to access these in your local library; if they're not available, your library may be able to borrow them through the 'Inter-Library Loan Network'. Your library may also belong to a group or consortium which will grant you access to other university libraries (for example the M25 group in the South East).

Libraries and Learning Centres

Your Students' Union card or a special library card will permit you access to various libraries on campus. Make time during Freshers' Week to locate these and familiarize yourself with the cataloguing system. The books are generally arranged by subject in a standard classification – the Dewey Decimal System is the standard used in libraries throughout the world (see Table 5.1). You should easily be able to find the relevant section and where your subject is kept in the library.

Almost all libraries have a computer database for locating books. You can make several different types of search on a database. If you know the author or title you can key these in and search. If you are just making a general inquiry about a subject to see what is available, you can type in a keyword and the database will provide you with a list of titles containing that word. There may well be a database on hard copy (as opposed to on computer) such as a microfiche system, or even index cards.

Table 5.1: Dewey Decimal System

000–099	General works
100–199	Philosophy and psychology
200–299	Religion
300–399	Social sciences
400–499	Languages
500–599	Pure sciences
600–699	Applied sciences
700–799	The arts
800–899	Literature
900–999	Geography, biography, history

When you first join you should be given an introduction on how the library works. If you are really stuck ask the library staff to help you – it's their job.

One of the main problems with university is that one textbook will suddenly be in demand by 100 students. Ascertain, if you can, what books may be relevant for the coming lectures and access them beforehand. Read them, take notes and make photocopies of relevant passages – this will also mean that you have some background knowledge and the lectures may be more intelligible and also more interesting. But do not write in the books.

A note on photocopying: this is usually dead cheap in the university library, but there may well be restrictions due to copyright laws. Check with the librarian how much of a text you can copy.

Some books may be restricted to use in the library only, whilst others may only be available to borrow for a very limited time. (This is to allow access by as many students as possible.) If you find that a text that you require has already been borrowed, you can ask the librarian to reserve it for you when it is returned. On the subject of returning books, keep aware of the dates they are due back, as you will incur library fines if you return them late. If you are a persistent offender, you may possibly have your library use restricted.

In these high-tech days the library will almost certainly offer information in other formats apart from books. These include audio and video tapes, CD-ROMs, periodicals and specialist journals, as well as possibly allowing you to log on to the Internet. With regard to the Internet, it is well worth taking advantage of any tuition available to show you how to use it in the most efficient way. Otherwise, you might find yourself surfing your study time away.

The library may also have a comprehensive backlist of previous students' theses and dissertations. These are a very useful resource if they cover your subject, but be very careful not to lift other people's work. The university authorities find plagiarism one of the most heinous crimes and can refuse to give you a degree. Ignorance is no defence, so be aware of your institution's plagiarism policy.

Apart from the main university library there are also often departmental libraries which will specialize in your subject. Your tutor or lecturers may also have a specialist collection of books in their field that they allow you access to. There may be public research libraries open to students in medium-sized and large cities. You can also join the local library. You will need to have ID and proof of where you are living. The local library will not offer the range of in-depth academic publications, although (as mentioned above) you may be able to order them on the Inter-Library Loan Network.

Tech Labs

These are offered as a resource to students who need to use a computer for part of their course. Nowadays most essays are expected to be presented in typed form, so access to a word processor is essential. Also, you may be required to e-mail your essays to your tutor. When you arrive at university you will probably be issued with an e-mail address. E-mail is particularly useful if your accommodation is far from the campus. (It is also an excellent way of keeping in touch with family and friends.)

Some sort of tuition will be available. Make sure you ask for help with your computer literacy. This is often offered free to freshers.

You are also expected to use the Internet for your research. This is a good resource if you know how to use it efficiently. You will be issued with some credits for printing off interesting and useful material (possibly 100 pages); thereafter you have to pay. When you need to access a terminal you will certainly have to queue, so take something to read.

Language students will have access to a language centre. You need to pay a small subscription, for which you get access to videos of news, satellite television, foreign films and newspapers, as well as the option to practise grammatical exercises.

Planning Your Time

> *One of the hardest things I found in my first year was that I suddenly had all this time. No-one seemed to expect me to do anything, so I didn't and I wasted hours and hours. I don't know what I did with it all.*

Apart from the preparatory reading for seminars, tutorials and lectures, you will also be required to submit essays and possibly dissertations for evaluation. The deadline may seem so far in the future (the following term) that it is easy to put it off and put it off. Then your plan to knock your work on the head during the vacation will fall by the wayside and suddenly you'll find that it's due in two days' time. You won't have done the necessary research and the texts won't be available (because several other students remembered the day before you about the assignment). So try to get on the case as soon as possible. Do your research, prepare your notes and plan the essay. This process is also easier if your essay or dissertation is relevant to a course of lectures which are still fresh in your mind. Actually writing the essay shouldn't take very long.

Making a Timetable

Find out at the beginning of term what commitments you will have on a regular basis – lectures, seminars, tutorials, clubs, a job, practicals etc. You can then set about drawing up a weekly timetable that will show you how much time you have to fit in your studying and your student pleasures.

When you draw up your timetable, it is best not to fill in every minute of the day; you won't be able to stick to it and the whole thing will become demotivating. Do try, however, to dedicate a regular time each week for studying and get into the habit of studying then. Also, review your position after a few weeks and dedicate more time if you are falling behind or change things if they are not fitting in with your way of life. For example, you might have joined the university wine-tasting society on Monday nights and find that four hours of study on Tuesday mornings is an unrealistic target. Reduce this and add in a bit more on Friday afternoon.

	09:00	10:00	11:00	12:00	13:00	14:00	15:00	16:00	17:00	18:00	19:00
Mon		lecture				lecture		library			
Tues	study					hockey practise					
Weds						study		tutorial			
Thu	seminar					library				fitness	
Fri		lecture		study		study					
Sat						hockey			clubhouse		

Note: this timetable does not include any part-time work commitments.

Figure 5.2: Timetabling your time

Figure 5.2 is a modest timetable but probably a reasonable starting point. Plenty of time hasn't been assigned so there is reasonable flexibility. It includes:

▓ 8 hours for lectures

▓ 9 hours of dedicated study

▓ 2 hours for a tutorial

▓ 2 hours for a seminar

- 5 hours in the library

- 8 hours of sport

- 2 hours of organized social time.

You may also find that it is worthwhile to draw up an overview of your termly commitments, as well as any key events to which you will be committed.

Table 5.3: Your termly commitments

Week	Commitment
One	–
Two	Essay
Three	First practical (results)
Four	Essay
Five	–
Six	–
Seven	Second practical (results)
Eight	Essay; seminar presentation; hockey tournament
Nine	–
Ten	Third practical (results)

By looking at this you know immediately that part of weeks five and six should be dedicated towards your commitments in week eight. If you prepare your essay and seminar then, rather than spending all the time (and grant) in the pub, then week eight will be enjoyable, especially if you do well in the hockey tournament. You can celebrate without having to stagger back to your room to attempt to focus on the swirling notes and figures for your seminar presentation the following afternoon.

Reading and Research

It was a real struggle to begin with. I had all these books to read and I couldn't understand any of them. They were so heavy.

Academic texts are hard to read. The language and vocabulary is difficult and you have to use your brain to understand them. Have a dictionary to hand (maybe even a technical dictionary) and note down any terms that you don't understand. You will find it easier to understand the texts as you become a more experienced reader.

During your degree you will be expected to collect, understand and analyse data. Much of this will depend on your own efforts and motivation.

There are a number of techniques that you can employ when reading texts for your course. It is important to decide exactly what information you require. Also you will be expected to carry out much more reading on your own initiative than you would have done for A-levels. Study-skills courses help you to understand these.

Skimming and Scanning

Skimming is used to ascertain what is in a book and whether it is relevant. Go through the book turning the pages quickly. Look at chapter headings, sub-headings, key points in bold print, photographs and illustrations. Note down points and page references that you feel are important. With scanning, you simply run through the chapter headings and the index, making similar notes of key pages and points to return to later.

Reading in Detail

Having selected what you feel are the important passages, you should go through the pieces several times. On your first run through you will just be finding what material it contains. If the subject-matter does not appear to be what you want, don't waste your time – find another text that is more helpful. However, if the information is good, read it through again more slowly and carefully. As you read it stop now and again and ask yourself questions about the meaning. Do you understand it? Do you agree with the inferences the author is making? If not, what do you think is the correct interpretation and why? When you have finished, close the book and write down the important points from memory.

Finally, go through it slowly again, filling in any points that you have missed and also extending your notes.

Keep asking yourself if you understand everything you read. It is also a good idea to pull out key quotations which will be useful for your essays. (Don't forget that these should always be used with the proper acknowledgement of the author.) Make sure that you head your notes with the name of the book and the author, the particular subject you are researching, the library reference, page numbers and chapter headings. This will make your life easier if you need to find the information again later on.

Taking Notes in Lectures

Making good notes is a skill you will acquire with a little practice. You should never try to write down everything – you will never succeed and you will not understand half of what is being said. Listen carefully to the lecturer and note down the key points that are raised. Hear what the lecturer has to say about these key points and ask yourself if you understand what she or he is driving at. You may also be given a bibliography or references to publications during the course of the lecture. Make a note of these as well.

Always write down the title of the lecture, the name of the speaker and the date. File them carefully by date and subject when you get home. It is also a good idea to review your notes shortly after the lecture to reinforce the knowledge that you have gained. The longer you leave it the less you will remember.

Essay Writing

When writing an essay, it is important to be thinking as clearly as possible and to feel comfortable with your grasp of the subject.

Read the essay title carefully and jot down any thoughts that you may have about what the question means and what information is being requested.

Now return to your sources, lecture notes, notes from tutorials and notes on texts. Find out as much information as you can and check that you have not forgotten any key points. Do not rely on one source for your essay; the tutor probably knows more about the subject than you ever will, and having one source gives you only one point of view.

When you are confident that you have gathered all the necessary data, you can write an essay plan, preferably from memory. You should have an introduction that outlines what you are hoping to prove, followed by the bulk of the information that you want to write (including quotations) arranged in a logical sequence of key points and finally the conclusion that you have reached.

You can now write the first draft of the essay. Leave the introduction and conclusion until the end. Start by filling out the key points from your essay plan. Go over this with your notes, checking facts and content. Keep asking yourself if what you are saying is relevant and that you are answering the question. Avoid being excessively verbose. University essays are about facts, information, analysis and argument. When you are happy with your first draft it is a good idea to leave it for a couple of days. It will then be easier to be objective when you read through it again. On your second read through, make corrections, take out any rubbish and add additional points that you feel are important. Carefully read through the introduction and conclusion and adjust them if necessary. Finally, produce the finished product on a word processor, checking through for your grammar, punctuation and spelling. Be careful if using a spell-check facility as these may have American spelling, a problem about which British academics can be a bit peculiar. The spell-check will also not pick up misspelled words if they look like other words; for example stationary/stationery and practise/practice.

When you have completed your essay, you will be required to draw up a bibliography. You may also be asked to annotate it with footnotes. Check with your tutor the style they desire.

Studying During the Vacations

Yes, they really expect you to work during the holidays. You will often be set reading assignments and essays to carry out. You'll probably say to yourself, 'No problem, I've got loads of time.' Wrong. Holidays tend to slip away very quickly. Work out how much time you think that the work is going to take you and programme it in at the beginning of the hols. You could stay up at university to do it. Then when you get home you can take up that part-time job, enjoy seeing your friends and family or go off on a trip without the cloud of the work hanging over you. Who wants to be studying in their room at the end of the vacation when all their friends are having goodbye drinks in the local?

Note: you can use your student card to access the libraries of other universities, although they won't let you borrow books.

Revision Techniques

Revising is a question of good organization and self-discipline. Check exactly what areas of study you are being examined on. There may well be some parts of your course that are not covered in the exam. Work out how much revision you need to do. Also, if for example in one paper you are only required to answer four questions out of a choice of eight topics, you will not need to revise all eight.

Leave yourself plenty of time in which to revise. Divide it up so that you have enough for each subject. Give yourself extra time for the subjects you are not confident about. Perhaps you could discuss these with your fellow students or your tutor. It is sometimes easier to talk over a subject than to just read about it.

Carry out your revision in a place where you can be free from interruption, maybe in the library. Or, if you are in your room, hang a 'Do not disturb on pain of death' sign and tell your flatmates that you are seriously working and completely unavailable for socializing.

Make yourself comfortable – but not too comfortable or you'll fall asleep during the grimmer passages – have good lighting and make sure all the material that you need is to hand before you start.

Once you begin don't overdo it – if you get tired nothing will stay in your brain. If you have decided to study for four hours divide it up with some breaks. Revise for an hour and 20 minutes, stop for coffee for 20 minutes, revise for an hour, go for a 20-minute walk, revise for an hour and stop. This will keep you fresher and help you to concentrate harder over the period. Also, promise yourself a reward. Promise yourself a curry or a trip to the cinema if you manage your four-hour programme for five days. Plan your time so that it suits you.

A good technique for revising is to transfer key points from your term's notes on to index cards and to go through them checking that you understand each point. If you have a problem go back to your notes and sources and work through them in more detail. Another method is to write out the key points on paper using bright markers to illustrate areas of different importance. In both these methods the act of transferring the notes is part of the process and will help you to visualize the information during an exam. You can also make a tape recording and listen to this several times. The difficulty of this method is retaining your concentration, especially if the subject is not very scintillating.

Exam Technique

During the revision period of the term it is also important to practise your exam technique. (Again, study-skills courses may offer this.) Use past papers and try to recreate the conditions of the examination hall. To get hold of past papers you will need to give your module code and the years of the papers that you want to the librarian. They will then copy them for a small charge. Don't leave this to the last minute as you may have to wait a while.

When you feel that you have assimilated the information from your revision, take an exam paper that you haven't eyeballed to the library. Sit yourself at a desk with all your exam paraphernalia and time yourself. Remember, no cheating if it is to be a valuable exercise. Start by reading the instructions to candidates carefully and make sure you know exactly how long you can allow for each question. Read through the paper and decide which questions you are intending to attempt. Allocate time for each answer.

Now plan your answers, like a quick essay plan. Sketch out the facts that you want to include and then think about your introduction and conclusion. For a half-hour answer, allow about 5–8 minutes to make your plan. Be careful to answer the question and not just write what you know about a similar or related subject. Also take care not to get carried away on one answer about which you feel particularly strong.

At various points during your mock exam give yourself a few minutes to collect your thoughts. Stretch, rest your writing hand and have something sweet to eat. Leave enough time at the end of the exam to read through your answers and correct any grammar and spelling, and to make sure you haven't put in any howlers.

Be strict with yourself and complete your exam within the allotted time. Now go and have a pint or a cup of tea before going over your answers with your revision notes to hand. Be harsh on yourself – you will probably discover areas in your subject on which you need to bone up a bit more.

Use these trial exams to build up your confidence and knowledge. Don't panic. Everyone will be suffering from some degree of exam stress, but a well-regimented revision schedule will go a long way to alleviating this. If you are completely stressed out, talk to your friends or personal tutor, or go and see the student counsellor. It is important not to get disabled by emotion.

The Exams Themselves

Before the examinations actually come round you must make sure of the following.

- You know the exact time and date.

- You know exactly where to go and how long it takes to get there.

- You know what topics are being covered.

- You know how long the exam lasts.

- You have all the equipment that you require and are permitted.

- You have new batteries in your calculator.

- Your pen is working and you have enough ink.

> You must take your student card or you may not be allowed to sit the exam.

If you are ill before the exam you should obtain a sick note from a doctor and inform the examiners before the exam.

They may upgrade your performance at their own discretion. Similarly, if you are unable to take the exam through illness it is important that the examiners know, beforehand if possible.

If you find that one exam is a disaster don't dwell on it. Try to think positively about the next one and tell yourself that you will do better. Anyway your judgement about your own performance is likely to be pessimistic. Good luck!

Some Common Problems and Solutions

You Find Yourself Struggling To Cope with Your Course

If this happens, or you cannot understand the lectures, it is easy to become despondent. It is best to deal with the problem as early as you can. Speak to your lecturers or tutor about it. They can offer you encouragement, point you towards the right source or even spend some time helping you through.

You Don't Like Your Course and Want To Change

The sooner that you decide this the better. It is possible to change your course, but you will need to have achieved good enough qualifications for the new course you want to do. There must be enough space on the new course as well. The first thing to do is to approach your tutor or director of studies and get them to agree to your change. It is also important to realize that if you leave it too late you may jeopardize your eligibility for your grant.

You Can Never Access the Texts That You Need for Your Course

It is possible to form a reading syndicate with other students on your course. You will then be able to share resources with them. If there are four of you, you will only need to obtain one text in four. A reading syndicate will require some degree of organization and cooperation for this to work.

You Keep Getting Disturbed By Your Flatmates When You Are Trying To Study

If your flatmates really don't respect the fact that you want to study you might want to look for alternative accommodation. You could have a word with the supervisor of the hall of residence, who might have a quiet word with the others. Alternatively, it might be enough to just go somewhere to study, the library, the faculty or maybe a friend's accommodation. This, of course, could also apply if you are still living at home with noisy younger siblings.

6 *Health Matters*

Don't be ridiculous. Scurvy is a sixteenth-century disease.

Being on your own for the first time, you will need to know how to take care of your health. You might also be required to do the odd spot of E.R. aid for your ailing flatmates.

If you have any doubts consult a professional.

Following a healthy regime is important for keeping healthy. You should try to eat a regular and balanced diet, making sure that your food is stored safely (see page 143). It is also advisable to take plenty of exercise (walking or cycling to lectures will do) and to make sure that you allow yourself enough sleep. This will help with not only your physical but also with your mental well-being.

Registering with the NHS and Charges

As soon as possible after your arrival you should register with a local GP or at the student medical centre. You will need to have your National Health card and the name and address of your previous family doctor. This will enable your new practice to obtain your medical notes. Information about this should be available during Freshers' Week or you can consult the public library or post office for a list of local doctors and other health facilities.

At the same time it is also worth trying to register with a dentist – you never know when that filling is going to fall out. Many dentists are reluctant to accept new patients registered under the National Health Service, so you may need to look around. The sooner you do this the better, as there are maybe 2,000 other potential patients out there trying to get on the list. Some universities have Schools of Dentistry where you can obtain free treatment.

Up to the age of 19, all your medical treatment costs are covered by the NHS. Thereafter you must register as a person on low income (shouldn't be a problem for a lowly undergraduate) to avoid prescription charges. To do this you will need to fill in form HC1 which you can pick up from your doctor, dentist, optician, local DSS office, NHS hospital or certain chemists. You should do this as soon as you are 19 and not wait until you need to shell out. The form can take a month or so to process. It takes even longer than this and is even more difficult to reclaim monies that you have already paid out. You can expect help towards:

▌ NHS prescription charges

▌ NHS dental treatment

▌ NHS wigs (for medical, not dramatic, purposes!)

▌ sight tests, spectacles and contact lenses

▌ travel costs to treatment.

These days many alternative therapies are respected by the medical profession and it may even be possible to get referred by your doctor and to receive free treatment.

Be careful, however. Whilst treatments such as acupuncture and osteopathy are recognised as beneficial, there are plenty of other alternative treatments whose provenance has not been properly studied but which are very effective at parting you from your money. Talk to your doctor before embarking on a week's course of Gingko Biloba and Guarana sensory-deprivation floatation baths or similar, when an aspirin might do the trick.

It is not a bad idea to put together a medical kit for your basic needs. You will almost certainly need it at some point during your degree. A basic medical kit is shown in Table 6.1.

Table 6.1: Student pharmacopoeia

Thermometer	*fever patrol*
Analgesic	*headaches and pains*
Alka seltzer	*Freshers' Week*
Antacid	*heartburn, acid indigestion*
Antiseptic cream or lotion	*cuts and scratches*
Plasters, various sizes	*blisters, cuts and scratches*
Arnica cream	*bruises*
Oil of cloves	*toothache relief*
Rescue remedy	*hangover*
Burn spray	*minor burns and scalds*
Liquid antiseptic	*antiseptic and throat gargle*
Lozenges	*relief for sore throats*
Hot-water bottle	*period pains, tummy ache*
Tweezers	*splinters*
Scissors	*to lose*
Cotton wool	*cleaning injuries*

Don't forget to have a supply of any regular medicines you may use (eg, inhalers, hay-fever tablets, skin creams).

Minor Ailments and How To Cope With Them

Headaches

There are a number of causes of headaches apart from excessive consumption of alcoholic beverages. One of the commonest causes is from bad posture. Studying in a bad position sets up tension in the muscles in your neck and shoulders that can give tension headaches. Anxiety and stress can also give you a headache.

Set up your desk so that you are in a proper position. Your feet should be flat on the floor, your back straight and supported at the bottom, and the keyboard and screen positioned so that you don't need to crane or twist your neck. Make sure that you have adequate lighting, as straining your eyes is also bad. Get up every so often to stretch and walk around.

Treatments include analgesic, massage, sleep and the Alexander technique.

Toothache

Usually caused by neglect. You should brush your pegs at least twice a day and you could also use a mouthwash. Try to avoid too many sweets, snacks and sweet drinks. Bring enough toothpaste from home – buying a new tube of 'Beaming Grin Dentipaste' often loses out in the battle with buying a pint at the Union.

Temporary relief can be provided by an analgesic or rubbing some oil of cloves on the painful part. A hot-water bottle wrapped in a towel and held to the face can also give some relief (don't forget to breathe). But go to a dentist as soon as possible. Once you've got toothache, it ain't going away. You should visit your dentist once or twice a year for a check-up. Remember, your smile is precious.

Earache

The most common cause of earache is an infection of the middle ear and often accompanies a cold, sore throat or flu. A couple of painkillers and the hot-water bottle treatment may offer some relief, but you will probably need to visit the doctor if it persists.

Coughs, Cold, Sore Throat, 'flu

A sore throat often marks the beginning of coughs, colds and 'flu. Drink plenty of fluids to ease the pain and stop your throat becoming dry. With coughs and colds there are a number of proprietary treatments for the symptoms available from the chemist, though it is well-known that there is no known cure for the common cold. You will be lucky if you don't go down with 'flu at least once during your undergraduate years. Make sure you have plenty of liquids – an isotonic drink is good, or orange juice which contains Vitamin C. Make sure you are warm enough, retire to bed and have plenty of sleep.

You may sometimes be offered inoculation against a particular strain of 'flu; this is fine as long as swine 'flu doesn't turn up when you've been inoculated against chicken 'flu. If you smoke, stop while you feel ill – you might quit for good.

If you have any doubts or worries about your symptoms, seek medical advice (see Meningitis).

Diarrhoea and Vomiting

This is your body's response to something it doesn't like. It is very often caused by food poisoning such as salmonella, over-indulgence at the bar, over-eating or eating very spicy foods. Or it might be due to an allergic reaction or set off by motion sickness. Diarrhoea and vomiting may occur singly or together.

One of the side-effects is that your body becomes dehydrated and loses many of its salts. You should make up a mixture of one litre of water, a teaspoon of table salt and five teaspoons of sugar and sip it slowly and often. Stick to bland foods such as plain toast or simply poached white fish for at least 24 hours.

If there is any evidence of blood or you are unable to keep anything down, seek immediate medical help.

Zits

Who needs 'em! They have an uncanny knack of coming to a head just before that incredible date you managed to arrange against all the odds. Diet seems to be important: avoid too many greasy foods, takeaways and too many sweeties, especially chocolate. Regular washing is important. There are various cleansing products on the market and they seem to help to a degree. Make sure that if you are wearing make-up, to clean your face thoroughly before going to bed. If it is really gruesome and getting you down go to the doc – some antibiotics may help.

The Blues

It is the nature of student life that you will feel down sometimes. Money, girl/boyfriend trouble, work pressure, family problems – all sorts of things can get to you. Provided it doesn't take control of your life and you get through it, no problem.

Exercise is very good for this, as is talking it over with your friends (who have probably experienced just the same problems). Or if this doesn't help you may want to talk to your personal tutor. The Students' Union has counsellors or can put you in touch with a therapist. There are anonymous helplines and of course your doctor may be able to help if your depression is very severe. One of the biggest problems is the apathy that is symptomatic of the condition. Just pushing yourself to try to begin to resolve the cause of the problem may actually be the first step on the road to recovery. A good mooch shouldn't last more than a couple of days.

Minor Injuries

Cuts and Scrapes

To deal with these, first of all wash your hands and dry them on a clean towel. Then rinse the wound under fresh running drinking water (usually only available from the kitchen cold tap.) Using some cotton wool soaked in antiseptic, clean any dirt, always wiping away from the wound. Pat the skin dry around the wound and cover with a dry sterile dressing.

If the wound becomes inflamed go to the doc. If the wound is caused by an animal, in a fight or is particularly dirty, you should have it checked out. You may need a tetanus shot. Remember, a sardonic grin is not precious. If a cut won't stop bleeding, or is very deep, you should go to the casualty department at your local hospital.

Bruises, Strains and Sprains

These are all varieties of soft-tissue injuries. The St John Ambulance suggest you follow the RICE procedure (see Table 6.2).

Table 6.2: The RICE procedure

R	Rest the injured part, supporting it steadily and comfortably.
I	Ice. Make a cold compress using a bag of ice or a bag of frozen peas and apply it to the injury to reduce the pain and swelling
C	Compress the injury using a crêpe bandage wound round quite tightly – but not a tourniquet.
E	Elevate the injury to reduce the flow of blood and reduce bruising and swelling.

Note: there are also several proprietary brands available over the counter for muscle strain. These are especially great for the jocks – the smell is so macho!

Serious Ailments To Recognize

Remember: if you have any doubts seek medical advice.

Meningitis

This insidious infection seems to like preying on students in a campus environment. There have been several outbreaks over recent years, usually in the autumn or spring. It is very serious. It can cause irreversible brain damage and is potentially fatal.

Rapid diagnosis and treatment are vital.

The symptoms, which develop very quickly, can be similar to flu. The symptoms include:

▓ headache

▓ vomiting

▓ stiffness in the neck

▓ fever

▓ convulsions

▓ photophobia (sensitivity to light)

▓ irritability

▓ purpuric rash of purple or red blood spots.

One of the tests is to press the rim of a glass over the rash. If the rash disappears under pressure it is not purpuric.

However, it is far better to leave the diagnosis up to the doctor. And if there is an outbreak, have the immunization offered. One of the biggest dangers is not diagnosing this sometimes fatal illness, as it often feels that you have a very bad hangover.

Appendicitis

This is caused when the appendix becomes inflamed through blockage or ulceration. Symptoms include severe pain in the abdomen (usually to the lower-right), nausea, vomiting, bad breath, fever and loss of appetite. If the appendix bursts it will lead to peritonitis. The usual treatment is the removal through surgery, and recovery is normally very swift.

Toxic Shock Syndrome

TSS is a blood-borne infection of the blood that has a destructive effect on the body's organs. It generally effects women who use tampons.

The symptoms include a high temperature, chills, headache, sore throat, decreased urine output and occasionally a peeling rash on the palms and the soles of the feet. It leads to lowering of the blood pressure followed by kidney failure and death.

Treatment is immediate hospitalization and removal of the tampon, intravenous antibiotics and blood pressure control.

Remember to change tampons at least every four hours.

Chronic Fatigue Syndrome (ME)

This condition is not fully understood, but it is thought to be caused by deficiency of the immune system, depression or as a result of severe viral infection.

Symptoms include fatigue, muscle pain, weakness, mild fever, chills, sore throat, tender lymph nodes, headache, sleep-pattern disturbance and mental confusion.

Treatment is usually by finding a balance of rest and general health maintenance. Depression may be a symptom or a cause and should be recognized and treated.

Scurvy

Aar ha, me hearty undergraduates, you really can get scurvy as we approach the twenty-first century. It is caused by bad diet, leading to a deficiency of Vitamin C in the body.

The symptoms include sore joints, perhaps with swelling, looseness of the teeth, bluish gums, slow healing of cuts, bruising of the skin and mucus membrane, fever, lack of energy and slowing of growth.

Increase your Vitamin C intake and the problem should go away. Drink orange juice, blackcurrant cordial mixed with cold water or rosehip syrup, or take Vitamin C tablets. (Excessive vitamin supplements are a waste of money as they pass straight through the body.)

Glandular Fever (Kissing Disease/mononucleosis)

Glandular fever is a viral infection with enlargement to the lymph glands.

As suggested by its other name, it is spread by kissing an infected person, or even drinking from the same glass. It is often found among student populations.

The symptoms are general malaise, tiredness, aching limbs, headaches, rash, sore throat, swollen lymph glands and tenderness of the liver.

Treatment includes plenty of rest, avoidance of alcohol, plenty of liquids, analgesia (pain relief) and good diet. It may take several weeks to clear up during which there can be more pronounced episodes. You will be infectious for weeks after which, you can resume snogging.

Sex: Sexually Transmitted Infections and Contraception

There have been plenty of awareness campaigns in recent years about the dangers of being infected with the HIV virus and the need to practise safe sex. HIV is only one of a number of infections that can be caught through engaging in penetrative sex (either vaginal or anal). Safe sex requires that you should always use a condom, even if other forms of birth control are being used. This is especially important if you have more than one partner or your partner is sleeping with others.

Whether you are male or female, it is up to you to be responsible for your own health and safety. In the hotbed of student life many sexual encounters are facilitated by the liberal consumption of alcohol. Your judgement may be impaired, so you should always carry a condom.

> *I'd had a condom in my wallet for so long it had worn a ring in the leather. I was depressed – I didn't know who was going to perish first – so I went down the pub to drown my sorrows. I'd almost decided that just carrying the thing doomed me to a life of celibacy. Then I got chatting to this girl, we had a few more pints and... well, I'm glad that I was prepared. I miss my old mate but I've got a new one now.*

It may seem promiscuous to be in a continual state of readiness for sex – but you wouldn't go out in the evening without your wallet, even if you didn't intend to spend any money. A passionate situation can develop at any time, and it is worth remembering that people with a sexually transmitted infection look completely normal.

You can obtain condoms free from the Family Planning Clinic, or they may be handed out on the campus.

Sexually Transmitted Infections (STIs)

HIV/AIDS

HIV (Human Immuno-deficiency Virus) is deadly. It affects the body's ability to defend itself against infection and leads to AIDS (Acquired Immune Deficiency Syndrome) and eventually to death. One of the main problems is that you may be infected and infectious for some time before you realize. In its earliest stages there are no discernible symptoms.

If you feel that you are at risk, it is possible to be tested at a genito-urinary medical clinic. You will almost certainly be given counselling before undergoing the test, as the effect of a positive result would be devastating. The test and its results are confidential and you do not even need to tell your GP.

HIV is spread by infected bodily fluids such as semen, pre-ejaculatory discharge, vaginal fluids, blood or urine entering into the bloodstream. This can happen during vaginal sex (particularly when the woman is menstruating) and during anal sex, when the weaker lining can be more easily ruptured. It can also be transferred by using a contaminated needle (see Chapter 7).

Oral sex using a condom is relatively safe, although it should be avoided if you or your partner have any cuts or sores around or in the mouth. If you are using sex toys they should be thoroughly cleansed before sharing.

Kissing is safe provided there are no open cuts or sores where bodily fluids could mingle.

If you are injured (especially if you know you are HIV-positive) you must be extremely careful there is no risk of your blood mixing with someone else's.

HIV virus does not survive very long out of the body and there is no danger of infection from touching someone or even drinking from the same cup.

Important: when you have sex with a new partner you will not and may never know their full sexual history. You should always practise safe sex. There is no cure for infection with HIV at present.

Chlamydia

Chlamydia is the most common STI and on the increase. It is particularly prevalent in women aged between 16 and 19 and men aged 20–24. However, 90 per cent of women and 25 per cent of men show no symptoms which means that it often goes undetected and spreads easily.

Symptoms for women include vaginal discharge, heavy bleeding between periods, low abdominal pain, abdominal pain during intercourse and pain when urinating. Symptoms for men are a discharge from the penis and pain when passing urine.

Chlamydia is easily treated with antibiotics but if left untreated can lead to Pelvic Inflammatory disease which can in-turn lead to infertility.

Gonorrhoea

This is caused by bacteria and is similar to, though less common than, chlamydia. Most women do not develop any symptoms.

Symptoms for men can include a discharge from the penis, burning pain when urinating and irritation and discharge from the anus.

Treatment is with antibiotics.

Syphilis

Syphilis is not very common in the UK today. It is caused by bacteria.

Symptoms are a painless sore on or near the penis, vagina or the mouth of the anus. Then a rash develops on the body along with 'flu-like symptoms. It should be treated as it can lead to heart problems and dementia.

It is treated with antibiotics.

Genital herpes

Most new cases of genital herpes are among 20–24 year olds. It is a viral infection and there is no cure.

The symptoms are a tingling or itching in the genital area, the appearance of small blisters, 'flu-like symptoms and a burning pain when passing urine.

Although there is no cure, the symptoms can be reduced in severity with an antiviral drug. Most people only have two or three attacks, although more are possible. You are most infectious when you have the blisters.

There is no cure available. Antiviral drugs can reduce the severity of the attack, although it can recur.

Genital warts

Genital warts are one of the most common STIs. They are caused by a virus and can recur. The highest rate of infection occurs among 16–19-year-old women and 20–24-year-old men.

They are not always visible and may take a year to develop after infection.

They can be treated with ointments, by freezing or removal by surgery under local anaesthetic.

Hepatitis B

This is caused by a virus and is spread through sexual contact (like HIV but more infectious). It can cause severe liver damage.

There is no specific treatment but it is possible to be vaccinated against the virus. Most people recover after a period of rest, and a total abstinence from alcohol.

Candidiasis (thrush)

Thrush is caused by a yeast infection often present in the vagina which multiplies to cause the symptoms. It can be triggered by some antibiotics or forms of contraception.

The symptoms for women are white vaginal discharge, itching, soreness and swelling of the vulva and pain when urinating. The symptom for men is a sore, inflamed, itchy penis.

The treatment includes vaginal pessaries and anti-fungal cream. Live yoghurt can also work.

Pubic lice (crabs) and scabies

These are small creatures that infest the pubic hair and can be spread by close body contact and sharing towels or bed linen as well as during sex. Pubic lice can spread to other parts of the body if untreated.

The symptom is severe itching. It can be treated with special cream or lotions.

Contraception (When You Don't Say No!)

> Condoms are the only contraceptive that offer protection against STIs or HIV and AIDS.

Condoms

Apart from providing some protection against infection, condoms also offer about 95 per cent protection against pregnancy. A number of surveys by the British Journal of Family Planning have shown that about half of all women with unwanted pregnancies were using condoms.

So remember that they are not foolproof.

Make sure that you use them correctly. If you think that you might be embarrassed at a critical moment practise putting a condom on privately. And a bit of humour during passion is no bad thing.

▓ Condoms are more effective if used with a spermacide, either jelly or pessary.

▓ Don't use oils or vaseline with male condoms as it damages them. Only use water-based lubricants.

▓ Make sure that you only use condoms with a British Kitemark (below).

Condoms are available free from Family Planning Centres and some genito-urinary medicine clinics. There are a number of varieties available: thinner for extra sensitivity, thicker which may help a man maintain an erection for longer, ribbed to give added sensation to the woman and flavoured for oral sex. Female condoms are also available, which gives women more personal control. Oil-based products can be used with a female condom. You can purchase condoms from a pharmacy. Also, many pubs and bars will have a machine in both the ladies and gents toilets. Sometimes they are handed out free on campus – don't be too shy to accept them.

The pill

There are two basic types of pill, a progesterone-only pill and an oestrogen/progesterone-combined pill. Different varieties of pill have different levels of the hormones and you will need to consult your GP or Family Planning Association before obtaining a prescription. You may need to try several varieties before finding one that suits you.

The progesterone pill works by making it difficult for the sperm to enter the womb or for the womb to accept a fertilized egg. The combined pill prevents ovulation.

The pill is taken every day for three weeks and then left for a week during which you will have your period. It is about 98 per cent effective, provided you follow the instructions. If you forget to take it you should take extra precautions. It is inadvisable to smoke if you are taking the pill. The pill may cause mood swings.

The pill offers no protection against STIs or HIV/AIDS.

Diaphragm or cap

A diaphragm is a flexible rubber device which is inserted into the vagina prior to sex. It covers the cervix and must be used in conjunction with a spermicide. It must be left in for at least six hours after intercourse.

It should be fitted for the first time by a doctor to ensure it is the correct size. It should be checked every year, or if you gain or lose more than three kg (seven lbs).

If it is inserted more than three hours before sexual intercourse, extra spermicide may be required. If used properly it is 92 per cent to 96 per cent effective.

The diaphragm does not provide any protection against STIs or HIV/AIDS.

Intra-uterine System (IUS)/Intra-uterine Device (IUD) – both are known as the coil

These are devices that are inserted into the womb by a doctor to prevent the sperm meeting the egg. They can also stop the egg from settling in the womb. They both begin working immediately.

The IUS is a plastic coil containing progesterone and can be useful for women who have heavy periods. It may cause irregular light bleeding for the first three months and side effects can include tenderness of the breasts and acne.

The IUD is a plastic and copper coil which can stay in the womb for five years. It may cause heavier, longer and more painful periods.

Both systems are at least 98 per cent effective.

The coil offers no protection against STIs, and HIV/AIDS.

> Note: the copper coil can be fitted up to five days after unprotected intercourse and prevents pregnancy in almost 100 per cent of cases.

Contraceptive injection

This is an injection which slowly releases the hormone progesterone into the body, preventing ovulation. It works for up to eight or twelve weeks.

Once you have had the injection it is irreversible, so that if you develop any side effects such as weight gain or irregular periods they may continue during the whole period that the injection is working. It is more than 99 per cent effective.

An injection offers no protection against STIs, or HIV/AIDS.

Hormone implant

Implants are small soft tubes which are surgically inserted under the skin of the upper arm. They provide a steady release of progesterone into the body, preventing the sperm from meeting the egg.

An implant can provide protection for up to five years. Temporary side effects include headaches and tenderness of the breasts, irregular periods and possible weight gain. Implants are more than 99 per cent effective. However they offer no protection against STIs or HIV/AIDS.

Natural methods (the rhythm method)

If this method is used according to the instructions it can be 98 per cent effective – but it's a very big IF. It works by calculating the fertile and infertile times of the menstrual cycle. To do this it notes different signs of ovulation or uses a contraceptive kit.

The advantages are that no hormones are used and that there are no side effects. It also gives a woman more awareness of her body. The disadvantages are that it is complicated, it is easy to make a mistake and you will still need to use other contraceptive methods if you have intercourse during the fertile part of your cycle. It also offers no protection against STIs or HIV/AIDS.

Pregnancy

You only need to have unprotected sex once to become pregnant. If you are fearful that you might have become pregnant it is possible to deal with it immediately using the morning-after pill (up to three days after sex) or a copper IUD (up to five days after sex).

However, you may not realize until after this period. Possible indications of pregnancy are missing periods, nausea and vomiting (morning sickness) and tenderness and enlargement of the breasts. You can buy a kit to test yourself form the local chemist or visit your doctor or Family Planning Centre.

It is important to deal with this as soon as possible. If you decide to continue with your pregnancy, you should visit your GP and make an appointment at the ante-natal clinic. On the other hand, if you decide that you might wish to terminate your pregnancy, the earlier you do it the safer it is. Abortions are available on the NHS but for a faster service there are private clinics where you will have to pay.

The Law on Abortion

In the United Kingdom, according to the Abortion Act, 1967 (amended by the Human Fertilisation and Embryology Act, 1990) legal termination of pregnancy may be carried out provided that two registered medical practitioners agree on the following.

Up to 24 weeks into the pregnancy

▓ The continuance of the pregnancy would involve a risk, greater than if the pregnancy were terminated, of injury to the physical or mental health of the pregnant woman or any existing children of her family.

The woman's actual or reasonable foreseeable future environment may be taken into account.

With no time-limits

▓ The termination is necessary to prevent grave permanent injury to the physical or mental health of the pregnant woman.

▓ there is a risk to the life of the pregnant woman, greater than if the pregnancy were terminated.

▓ There is a substantial risk that if the child were born it would suffer from such physical or mental abnormalities as to be seriously handicapped.

> **Note:** the 1967 abortion act does not extend to Northern Ireland where abortion is not available on the NHS or privately, except in exceptional circumstances, such as to save the mother's life.

Tits and Bollocks – Men's and Women's

Testicular Cancer

Cancer of the testicles is most prevalent among men aged 20–40. It is therefore important that you are aware of what is normal for you and to check regularly. If you feel any lumps or experience any pain you should make an urgent appointment with your doctor. Though this usually turns out to be innocuous, it is essential to be absolutely certain in case any treatment is required. If it is, it should be started immediately.

Breast Cancer

Similarly for women, awareness and regular examination of the breasts is essential. You should know what is normal for you and inspect your breasts every month, ideally one week after your period.

Look at them in the mirror and feel them all over with a flat hand. If you detect any lumps or notice any changes – pain, discharge from the nipple or change in skin texture– report it at once to your doctor. Nine out of ten lumps are not cancerous but don't take any chances.

Cervical Smears

The Department of Health recommend that women should have a smear test at least once every five years. Your doctor will arrange this. It may be more frequent if she is prescribing contraception to you. It is a quick, rather unpleasant (though painless) procedure, during which a sample is scraped from the cervix and sent for analysis. This screening is important so that any problems can be diagnosed and dealt with early.

Cystitis

Cystitis is an inflammation of the bladder of women. It can be very itchy and irritating.

Treatment can be by mixing four teaspoons of bicarbonate of soda with four pints of water and steadily drinking this in the course of the day. If the symptoms persist you should seek medical advice.

Useful Contacts

British Acupuncture Council
Park House
206–208 Latimer Road
London W10 6RE
0171 834 1012

British Homeopathic Association
27A Devonshire Street
London W1N IRJ
0171 935 2163

Family Planning Association UK
2–12 Pentonville Rd
London N1 9FP
0171 837 4044

Family Planning Association Cymru
4 Museum Place
Cardiff CF1 3BG
01222 342 766

Family Planning Association Scotland
Unit 10
Firhill Business Centre
Firhill Road
Glasgow G20 7BA
0141 576 5088

Family Planning Association Northern Ireland
113 University Street
Belfast BT7 1HP
01232 325488

Institute for Complementary Medicine
PO Box 194
London SE16 1QZ
0171 237 5165

Marie Stopes International
108 Whitfield Street
London W1P 6BE
0171 388 4843

National AIDS Helpline
0800 567 123

British Pregnancy Advisory Service
11–13 Charlotte Street
London W1P 2HD
0171 637 8962

Terence Higgins Trust
52–54 Gray's Inn Road
London WC1 8JU
0171 242 1010
(AIDS helpline available from 12 noon to 10pm).

7 Higher Education About Drugs and Alcohol

Man I was wasted so much of the time – I nearly failed my first year exams.

Drugs and Health

Using drugs carries a range of physical and mental health risks, and the only certain way to eliminate these is not use them at all. You may not feel this is realistic when the decision to use or not to use a particular drug is your personal choice. But you must acknowledge that when choosing to use a drug you accept the associated health risks. Within the student environment there will always be plenty of opportunities to use or experiment with drugs. This chapter is aimed at letting you know what the effects, risks and legal consequences of partaking are.

Don't be tempted to try something because of peer pressure. Understand what may happen and make your own choice.

Types of Drugs

Drugs can be categorized in many ways: hard or soft, uppers or downers, addictive or non-addictive, most harmful or least harmful, legal or illegal. One way of dividing drugs is by their effects.

Stimulants

These increase the activity of the central nervous system.

Examples: amphetamines, anabolic steroids, caffeine, cocaine, crack, ecstasy, poppers and tobacco.

Hallucinogens

These alter perceptions of reality and may result in hallucinations (seeing something that is not there).

Examples: cannabis, magic mushrooms and LSD.

Depressants

These reduce the activity of the central nervous system.

Examples: alcohol, Codeine, distalgesic, Gees Linctus, heroin, pethidine, solvents and minor tranquillisers (eg Valium).

Health Risks To Do with Drugs

Injecting drugs directly into your bloodstream carries some very serious health risks.

- There is a risk involved where the injection is not carried out correctly: puncturing an artery or allowing air into your bloodstream.

- If the equipment used to inject (needles, syringes, spoons, filters, etc.) is not clean, or is shared with other users, there are risks of tetanus, hepatitis B and C, HIV and other blood-borne infections.

- The impurities, ranging from rat poison to talcum powder, that are without doubt mixed with any street drug may cause allergic or toxic reactions with unpleasant short-term symptoms, and can also block veins and infect injection sites, causing septicaemia and abscesses.

Drugs can cause physical, psychological, social and legal problems.

▓ With some drugs the user may become psychologically dependent – this means they feel life is impossible unless they continue to use the drug.

▓ With some drugs the user may become physically dependent – this means their body experiences unpleasant physical symptoms if they suddenly stop using the drug.

▓ With some drugs the user may become both psychologically and physically dependent.

Legal Consequences

It is a common myth that some areas have an amnesty for people caught in possession of drugs. As with all crimes, the police will handle each case on its own merits. Be warned – possession can lead to imprisonment and heavy fines.

The interpretation of who is a 'dealer' or supplier of these drugs is made by the police and the courts and depends on the individual. Even if you are dealing 'not for profit', supplying drugs carries heavy penalties.

The Misuse of Drugs Act states the maximum penalties for:

▓ possession (having the drug)

▓ supplying (including intending to supply, giving away, selling, sharing, bartering, etc) certain drugs.

Drugs are listed as Class A, B or C. Some of these are shown in Table 7.1.

If you are sentenced in a crown court, the maximum penalties for supplying Class A and B drugs can be life or 14 years' imprisonment respectively, an unlimited fine or both.

You may be surprised to learn that it is an offence for the owner or somebody concerned with the management of any premises to allow the production or supply of a Class A, B or C drug, or the smoking of cannabis. So if you invite friends back to your flat, and you know they are sharing a controlled drug but do nothing to stop them, you have committed an offence.

Table 7.1: Maximum penalties in a magistrates' court for some drugs

Drug	Possession	Supply
Class A (cocaine, crack, heroin and other strong opiates such as methadone; ecstasy, LSD, and hallucinogenic mushrooms if dried or processed)	6 months' imprisonment, £5,000 fine or both	6 months' imprisonment, £5,000 fine or both
Class B (barbiturates, cannabis leaf and resin, codeine and mild opiates, eg DF118s; any Class B drug designed for injection counts as Class A)	3 months' imprisonment, £2,500 fine or both	6 months' imprisonment, £5,000 fine or both
Class C (anabolic steroids and tranquillizers, ie benzodiazepines, Valium, Temazepam, etc)	3 months' imprisonment, £1000 fine or both	3 months' imprisonment, £1000 fine or both

The maximum penalties in a magistrates court for this offence are:

▓ Class A or B drug: 6 months' imprisonment, £5,000 fine or both

▓ Class C drug: 3 months' imprisonment, £2500 fine or both.

If you are sentenced in a crown court, the maximum penalties for supplying class A and B drugs can be life or 14 years imprisonment respectively, or an unlimited fine, or both.

Academic and Career Consequences

In some cases being in the same room as someone taking or supplying drugs can lead to problems. It is not just a criminal record and heavy fines that students need to be aware of when engaging in any activities that involve drugs. Most universities and colleges will expel students from their premises if caught in possession of, taking or supplying drugs. This can mean that if caught you could be homeless very quickly, with no favourable reference for future accommodation. Furthermore, universities and colleges may inform the police, not to mention throw you off your course of study. This again would make it very hard to apply successfully for a course of education at another college or university. Drug conviction can also create difficulties when applying for some travel visas.

Students should be aware that, increasingly, employers are introducing mandatory drug tests for potential employees. Some drugs can stay in the body for a month or more – students should be aware of the implications of taking illegal drugs.

People's attitudes to drugs vary and not everyone may share your opinions, so what some may think is harmless recreational drug use may be seen by friends or family members as a serious breach of the law and carry heavy moral judgements. So it is worth bearing in mind all these factors before you engage in any activity that involves illegal drug use.

It is also becoming increasingly widely accepted that driving a car when under the influence of a drug can severely effect your ability. The police are currently carrying out an experimental series of roadside drug tests to ascertain if their equipment is reliable. It seems likely that these will become legal if the programme is acceptable. The effects of taking a drug may take more than 24 hours to wear off.

The advice is not to risk yourself or your friends by driving after drug use.

Alcohol (a.k.a Booze, Liquor) – The Most Popular Student Drug

Jamie was drinking so much the first term that he started having the shakes each morning and when he went to the doctor he was diagnosed as having become dependent on alcohol – in other words, he had become an alcoholic.

Beer and wine drinking almost certainly predate recorded history and are an integral part of everyday life in Britain. However, at university, where so much of the social life takes place in the pub, students often find themselves drinking a lot more than they ever have before.

Highs

Alcohol is absorbed into the bloodstream and starts to take effect within five to ten minutes. Effects may last from one to several hours, depending on the dose. The effects can vary according to body size, whether food is in the stomach and how much the person is used to drinking. After the equivalent of drinking two pints of beer most people feel less inhibited and more relaxed. Jovial and merry feelings can occur and getting drunk is a relatively common event, especially in student circles.

Lows

The first negative effect most people will experience with alcohol is a hangover, consisting of one or more of a variety of symptoms, including a headache caused by dehydration (alcohol affects the pituitary gland that controls the flow of water released by the body through urine). A sick and raw feeling of the stomach can occur. Whilst under the influence of alcohol accidents can occur and alcohol should not be taken before or while operating machinery or driving (even if you drank the night before). Larger doses of alcohol may lead to depressive and violent behaviour. The sex drive may increase but performance may suffer, one form being 'brewers droop'. Alcohol is packed with calories: one gin and tonic contains the same amount of calories as a bowl of ice-cream, so consistent use can lead to noticeable weight gain.

Alcohol does not mix with other drugs

It is not a good idea to take alcohol with other drugs as it can exaggerate the effect of those drugs. There are risks of overdosing, becoming unconscious and choking on one's vomit, which can result in death. It is worth remembering that many drug-related deaths occur through mixing alcohol with other drugs.

Long-term Effects

For some students alcohol consumption increases without them realising. This can result in financial problems and hangovers and affect their ability to concentrate on their studies – morning lectures are missed and they find themselves having to fit their lifestyle around their alcohol use. Some of these students may even experience health problems, such as early gastric and liver damage.

Regular drinking of large amounts of alcohol by pregnant women can harm the foetus. Both physical and psychological dependence may occur with high levels of use.

Legal Status

The production, distribution, consumption and sale of alcohol are controlled by various laws and regulations. Alcohol can only be sold from licensed premises. The license is awarded by local Magistrates generally in full 'on-licences', eg pubs where alcohol can be drunk on the premises, or 'off licences' where the alcohol cannot be consumed on the premises. Restaurants may be licensed to permit the drinking of alcohol accompanied by a meal. The times alcohol may be sold are also restricted, although these are more relaxed in Scotland. You can make your own wine and brew your own beer but it is illegal to make spirits.

Amphetamine Sulphate (a.k.a. Amphetamines, Whizz, Berwick, Speed, Sulphate)

There is no standardized quality of amphetamines or any other illegal drug. It may be cut with a variety of impurities such as talcum powder and as a result it is rarely more than five per cent pure when sold on the street. The drug comes in the form of a coloured or off-white powder and is packaged in a 'wrap' made from an envelope of folded paper. It can be taken by snorting, swallowing, drunk with juice or by injecting. It is usually sold by the gram.

Highs

Amphetamines cause the user to feel more confident, talkative and cheerful. Concentration is increased but usually only for single repetitive tasks. It is also used in clubs as a dance stimulant.

Lows

Short-term effects include an increase in breathing and heart rate, dilation of the pupils and suppression of appetite. As amphetamines are cut with a variety of impurities it is particularly dangerous to inject. To users, their thinking may seem clearer, but to the non-user they may appear to have 'verbal diarrhoea' or be over-fidgety. After the effects have worn off, the user may feel tired, anxious, irritable and restless. High doses can produce panic and even hallucinations.

Long-term Effects

These include weakness due to lack of sleep and food and lowered resistance to disease. There may also be delusions, hallucinations, paranoia and amphetamine psychosis (severe mental disorder). Amphetamines do not produce physical dependence, but users may become psychologically dependent and upon stopping may experience intense depression.

Legal Status

Amphetamine sulphate is a Class B controlled drug, (Class A if designed for injection). Some amphetamines are prescribed. Otherwise it is illegal to possess, supply or produce, (unless authorised to do so). Similarly it is illegal to allow premises to be used for the supply or production of amphetamines.

Alkyl Nitrites (a.k.a Poppers — Sold Under The Brand Names of Rush, TNT, RAM, etc)

These are a group of chemicals which include amyl nitrite, butyl nitrite, and isobutyl nitrite. They generally come in small bottles with screw tops or plug tops, as a clear yellow liquid with a sweet smell when fresh. They are available in sex shops, clubs and bars.

Highs

They are mostly used as a dance enhancer on the club circuit but can also be used as a muscle relaxant and sexual stimulant. It is usually sniffed directly from the bottle and once inhaled, effects last for two to five minutes. The effect is a head rush similar to hyperventilation as the blood vessels dilate, the heart rate increases and blood rushes to the brain.

Lows

Reduced blood pressure could lead to unconsciousness. Heart attacks have been recorded but no fatalities have been reported. Users often experience weakness, headaches, nausea and vomiting. The effects are increased if mixed with other drugs. Regular use can lead to skin complaints, sometimes accompanied by swelling of the nasal passages. This substance is highly dangerous if swallowed and can lead to death. Alkyl Nitrites have not been reported as causing any dependence.

Long-term Effects

There have not been any reports of additional adverse consequences resulting from long-term use.

Legal Status

Alkyl Nitrites are medicinal products and are controlled by the Medicines Act, 1968. Possession is not an offence, but it is illegal for anybody except doctors and chemists to produce or supply them, (unless authorized to do so).

Anabolic Steroids (Durabolin, Stanozol, Dianabol)

Steroids are derived from hormones that occur naturally in the body and are responsible for the development and function of the reproductive organs. These anabolic steroids promote the build-up of muscle tissue and are used by some athletes and body builders. Most synthetic anabolic steroids on the market are derived from human testosterone. However some are intended for use on animals and should not be consumed by humans.

Highs

Users report that steroids help them recover more easily from strenuous exercise. It has also been claimed that steroids enhance athletic performance.

Lows

Research indicates that the use of anabolic steroids results in aggression, stunted growth in young people, increased blood pressure and abnormalities in body development (this can apply to both men and women users).

Long-term Effects

For some users psychological dependence may occur.

Legal Status

Anabolic steroids are Class C controlled drugs. Some anabolic steroids may be prescribed. Otherwise they are illegal to supply or produce (unless authorized to do so). Similarly it is illegal to allow premises to be used for their supply or production. It is legal to possess them without a prescription if they are in the form of a medicinal product.

Barbiturates (a.k.a. Barbs, Downers)

These calm people down and in higher doses act as sleeping pills. They come in many forms and are usually taken orally but may be injected. They are only prescribed for treating severe insomnia.

Highs

A small dose makes the user feel relaxed and a larger dose puts the user to sleep. The effects are exaggerated by taking alcohol – this results in intoxication.

Lows

Overdosing can easily occur. Alcohol contributes to overdosing. Large overdoses cause death.

Long-term Effects

Both physical and psychological dependence may occur.

Legal Status

Barbiturates are Class B controlled drugs (Class A if designed for injection). Barbiturates may be prescribed. Otherwise they are illegal to possess, supply or produce (unless authorized to do so). Similarly it is illegal to allow premises to be used for their supply or production.

Benzodiazepines (a.k.a Valium, Temazepam, Librium, Mogadon, Jellies, Bennies)

These are one of the most commonly prescribed drugs for sleeping and anxiety problems. They are available as pills and capsules and are taken orally, but are also injected.

High

They reduce feelings of tension and increase feelings of calmness.

Lows

The body soon develops a tolerance to them, so a person has to take more to achieve the same effect. Both physical and psychological dependence can occur.

Long-term Effects

Both physical and psychological dependence will occur with most users of Benzodiazepines.

Legal Status

Benzodiazepines are Class C controlled drugs. Benzodiazepines may be prescribed. Otherwise it is illegal to supply or produce them (unless authorized to do so). Similarly it is illegal to allow premises to be used for their supply or production. It is legal to possess them without a prescription (if they are in the form of a medicinal product). However it is an offence to possess Temazepam without prescription.

Caffeine

In its purest form, caffeine is a white powder. It is found in coffee, tea, many soft drinks such as colas and energy drinks and over the counter painkillers. Coffee contains the most caffeine, especially when percolated. Most adults consume 440mg of caffeine per day. Painkillers which contain caffeine usually have 50mg per tablet. It is possible to double one's daily dose if these are consumed on top of a daily caffeine intake.

Highs

Caffeine stimulates the nervous system, counters tiredness and helps to prevent boredom.

Lows

In the short term, larger doses of caffeine impair performance, especially where attention to detail or delicate tasks are required. Anxiety, increased heart rate and blood pressure can occur with moderate doses. Larger doses can cause anxiety and restlessness, chronic insomnia and heart palpitations. Withdrawal symptoms include fatigue, lack of alertness, drowsiness and irritability. Although physical and psychological dependence may occur, medical assistance is not required.

Long-term Effects

There is no long-term effect from using caffeine.

Legal Status

Caffeine is not subject to any legal restrictions.

Cannabis (a.k.a. Blow, Puff, Dope, Hash, Grass)

This is the most commonly used illegal drug in the UK. It is usually smoked in the form of resin, a brown solid mass which is crumbled and mixed with tobacco to form a joint or spliff. Alternatively cannabis can be taken orally whether raw or mixed in cakes, cookies or fudge.

It can also come in its original leaf form (grass) and as an oil.

Highs

The effects of cannabis vary from person to person. Some users may feel more talkative, more relaxed and experience a sense of well-being and of being 'stoned' (heightened perception), often mentally distancing them from their surroundings. Mild hallucinations and strong feelings of affection may occur. 'Skunk' is a new strain of cannabis that is extremely potent, causing very strong hallucinogenic experiences.

Lows

Short-term effects include the following. When smoked cannabis contains carcinogenic chemicals. If a joint is made using cannabis and tobacco this will cause even more damage to the lungs. The most common bad reactions to cannabis are anxiety, paranoia, panic attacks, mood swings, sleeping problems, short-term memory loss and reduced concentration, which can be dangerous if operating machinery or driving. Furthermore, cannabis can result in a craving for food which could lead to noticeable weight gain with continuous use.

Long-term Effects

Cannabis may bring to the surface in some users emotional problems which may lead to more severe mental health problems. Heavy users may become demotivated in life and lose interest in academic matters. Users may begin to change their lifestyle to fit around taking cannabis and lose interest in their friends, family and social affairs.

Like tobacco, long-term regular smoking can lead to bronchitis and other lung diseases such as lung cancer. Physical dependence does not occur, although psychological dependence may.

NB Traces of cannabis can stay in the body for at least a month. This could be an issue if a user has to take a pre-employment medical examination.

Legal Status

Cannabis leaf and resin is a Class B controlled drug. Cannabis oil can be either a Class A or Class B controlled drug, depending on how the oil is produced. It is illegal to possess, supply, produce or cultivate cannabis (unless authorized to do so). Similarly, it is illegal to allow premises to be used for the supply or production or smoking of cannabis.

Cocaine (a.k.a. Charlie, snow, coke) and Crack (a.k.a. Rock, Stone, Wash)

Cocaine comes in the form of a white powder made from the coca shrub that can be eaten, smoked, sniffed or injected. Crack is derived from cocaine hydrochloride. It too is white, but in the form of crystals or rocks the size of raisins that are smoked.

Highs

The user can feel invincible and confident due to a powerful buzz. Animated and intense talking and feelings of well-being and strength are common, as well as a preoccupation with the effect of the drug. The intense high lasts ten to fifteen minutes. The remaining effects disappearing within an hour. As a result the user may need repeated doses to maintain the high. The user may feel a constant need for more to obtain the same effect.

Lows

Short-term effects include anxiety, hallucinations and feelings of persecution, and the sensation of bugs under the skin followed by tiredness, hunger and depression. Users may become psychologically dependent.

Strong psychological dependence may occur with crack users. Its short-lived effect can lead to a habit which is very expensive to maintain.

Long-term Effects

Withdrawal is very difficult. Regular users can experience the high being replaced with tiredness, depression, sickness, restlessness and weight loss. The lining of the nose can be damaged from sniffing the drug.

Legal Status

Cocaine and crack are Class A controlled drugs. Cocaine may be prescribed in certain circumstances. Otherwise it is illegal to possess, supply or produce (unless authorized to do so). Similarly it is illegal to allow premises to be used for their supply or production.

Ecstasy (a.k.a. E)

This is the name for tablets or capsules containing the drug Methylenedioxlmethylamphetamine (MDMA). Ecstasy may be sold under a variety of names such as Snowballs, Doves, New Yorkers, Burgers, etc. Each different sort of tablet has slightly different effects. Ecstasy is mainly taken orally. However, it can also be snorted, or, more rarely, injected.

Highs

Ecstasy starts to take effect after approximately 30 minutes and its effect could last for several hours. If there is no effect after 30 minutes another dose should not be taken. Different users are affected in different ways, some experiencing an urge to dance or be affectionate with people around them.

Users may experience a feeling known as 'coming up' where the drug sends rushes all over the body and brain producing a feeling of 'ecstasy'. These may include a tingling feeling in the spine and an overall feeling of joy. Slight hallucinations may also occur. Do be aware that ecstasy makes some people more likely to end up having sex, so be prepared and carry and use a condom if the occasion arises.

Ecstasy acts like a stimulant so those with heart conditions, respiratory conditions and/or epilepsy should definitely not take it. Aches, pains, muscle stiffness, spasms and twitching, cramps, vomiting, stomach ache, dizziness, panic attacks and depression, temporary paranoia and insomnia are all after-effects of taking ecstasy. Continuous dancing in hot venues may result in dehydration. This can be avoided by drinking up to a maximum of one pint of water (or other still soft drinks) per hour. Excessive consumption of liquids can be dangerous and should be avoided. Physical dependence does not occur, but psychological dependence is possible.

Ecstasy has been linked to deaths concerning young people. Regular use depletes an essential brain chemical, serotonin. This can lead to depression.

Legal Status

Ecstasy is a Class 'A' controlled drug. It can not be prescribed and is illegal to possess, supply or produce. Similarly it is illegal to allow premises to be used for its supply or production.

Hallucinogenic Mushrooms (Liberty Cap, Fly Agaric) (a.k.a. Magic Mushrooms)

These mushrooms grow in many parts of the country. They contain hallucinogenic substances called psilocin and psilocybin. Magic mushrooms come in various forms and strengths and therefore there is no set amount to be eaten, as results will vary.

Highs

Experiences will vary from visions of beauty to heightened awareness of sound and colour.

Lows

A danger comes from picking the wrong kind of mushrooms, which may be poisonous and can be fatal if ingested. If there are any doubts about the identity of any mushrooms they should not be consumed. Poisoning can take up to 40 hours to develop. Anyone feeling ill after taking mushrooms within this period should consult a doctor immediately. If possible, samples of the mushrooms and any vomit should be taken to the doctor to help identification of the poison consumed. Effects may include dizziness, depression, disorientation and sometimes panic.

Long-term Effects

The main danger is to people who have or are unaware they have a mental illness, as the drug can bring on symptoms of the illness. Hallucinogenic mushrooms may in any event trigger a psychotic response. Users may also experience a 'flashback' where the trip is relived some time after taking any mushrooms. Physical dependence does not occur, but psychological dependence is possible. Some mushrooms may contain worms which can be passed on to the user!

Legal status

There are no restrictions on possessing, supplying or cultivating magic mushrooms if they are in their natural raw state. However, they become illegal if dried, processed or prepared in any way, as this has been held by the courts to result in the preparation of psilocybin or psilocin which are Class A controlled drugs.

Heroin (a.k.a. Smack, Junk, Gear)

Heroin is a depressant drug derived from the opium poppy and is used medically for controlling extremely severe pain. However, the heroin which is sold illegally is cut with impurities like talcum powder, glucose and flour to increase the bulk and increase profit. It comes in the form of white or light brown powder and is sold in small paper wrappers.

Heroin can be sniffed or smoked or the powder can be dissolved in water and injected. Any drug is dangerous when injected and death from overdose is possible. Injecting with unclean shared needles can be hazardous to the user's health because of the danger of transmitting HIV, hepatitis and other diseases.

Highs

Heroin depresses brain activity including reflexes like coughing, breathing and heart rate. The drug takes effect almost immediately and the effects can last several hours, depending on the dose. Contentment, relief from stress and a warm pleasant drowsiness may all be felt by the user.

Lows

For the non-regular user there can be immediate unpleasant effects like nausea and vomiting, which will often deter someone from using the drug again. Overdosing on heroin can cause unconsciousness and may result in death from breathing failure or inhaling vomit.

Long-term Effects

When used regularly the effects cause a high followed by 'withdrawal' (sweating, jitters, diarrhoea, vomiting and cramps). If taken frequently, the user starts to increase the dose to get the same effect. Psychological and physical dependence often occurs. It can take years to get free of heroin. Regular use leads to poor health due to bad diet and chaotic lifestyle. Female users' menstrual cycles may become disrupted.

Legal Status

Heroin is a Class A controlled drug. In its medicinal form heroin may be prescribed in certain circumstances. Otherwise it is illegal to possess, supply or produce (unless authorized to do so). Similarly it is illegal to allow premises to be used for the supply or production of heroin.

Lysergic Acid Diethylamide (a.k.a. LSD, Acid, Trips, Tabs)

Acid is an hallucinogen which usually comes in the form of impregnated paper squares which may have colourful designs on them. LSD squares or 'tabs' are taken orally.

Highs

After taking LSD, the user may experience intense and changeable emotions and the senses behave in unexpected ways, eg visions and an 'understanding' of the universe, etc. Users may experience heightened self-awareness and a feeling of being outside their body. The effect (or trip) lasts up to eight to twelve hours, depending on the dose. Experiences will vary from visions of joy and beauty to heightened awareness of sound and colour.

Lows

In the short term LSD is not physically addictive. Effects depend to some extent on the user's mood and may include dizziness, depressions, disorientation and sometimes panic. It is normal to feel tired, drained of energy and confused for some time afterwards. The main danger may be to people who have or are unaware they have a mental illness, as the drug can bring this on. LSD in any event may trigger a psychotic response.

Long-term Effects

Users may experience a 'flashback' where the trip is relived, possibly years after taking it. Physical dependence does not occur but psychological dependence is possible.

Legal Status

LSD is a Class A controlled drug. It cannot be prescribed. It is illegal to possess, supply or produce. Similarly it is illegal to allow premises to be used for its supply or production.

Solvents

Solvents are chemicals found in substances like glue, paint, aerosols, Tippex and Butane Gas and are generally sniffed or inhaled. When inhaled some of them have effects similar to alcohol.

Highs

The user may feel giddy, light-headed and drowsy and in some cases hallucinate.

Lows

Short-term effects are that breathing and heart rate are depressed. Repeated or deep inhalation can cause disorientation, loss of control and loss of consciousness. Effects disappear within a few minutes to half an hour after sniffing. Afterwards the user may experience a mild hangover (headaches and poor concentration) for about a day. Sniffing carries the risk of death through choking on vomit. About 100 deaths occur every year, usually due to freezing of the lungs or suffocation. As with alcohol, accidental death by injury can occur.

Long-term Effects

Heavy use over several years may result in lasting damage to the brain, affecting control of movement. Long-term damage to the kidneys and liver can also occur. Long-term users will have the hangover symptoms of paleness, tiredness, forgetfulness and lack of concentration. Performance and function may be affected and weight loss, depression and trembling may occur; but these will disappear when the sniffing has stopped. Psychological dependence may occur and there have been reports of physical dependence.

Legal Status

The possession of solvents is legal. However, in Scotland the use of solvents for intoxication may be considered grounds for putting those under 18 in care. Otherwise the only restriction in the UK is that it is an offence to supply solvents to someone under 18 if the supplier believes they are likely to use them to achieve intoxication.

Tobacco

This is the dried leaves of the tobacco plant. It grows in many parts of the world. Tobacco can be consumed in cigarettes, cigars and pipes, chewed, or sniffed in the form of snuff. Approximately 30 per cent of people aged 16 and over regularly smoke. Most tobacco is smoked in the form of cigarettes.

Highs

Cigarette smoke contains various substances such as nicotine, tar, carbon monoxide and other gases. Some of these substances are absorbed by the lungs. Nicotine is the active addictive ingredient of cigarette smoking as it builds up in the body. The effects decline soon after stopping. As a consequence, the user may be left wanting more after only a short time. One or two cigarettes will increase blood pressure and heart rate. The appetite will be suppressed and the skin's temperature will lower. Smokers can use cigarettes to relieve tension, boredom and tiredness. First-time users may feel dizzy and slightly sick.

Lows

The more you smoke the more you are at risk from heart disease, lung cancer, blood clots, heart attacks, bronchitis and many, many more serious diseases. It may affect your skin complexion. When smokers stop they may experience withdrawal effects such as restlessness, irritability and depression. Physical and psychological dependence often occurs with regular use. During pregnancy smoking should be avoided as it leads to an increased risk of miscarriage and smaller baby weight.

Long-term Effects

Tobacco contributes to at least 100,000 deaths each year in the UK. A quarter of young male smokers will die 'before their time' due to smoking-related diseases. Smoking tobacco can cause irreversible damage to the lungs. However, if no irreversible damage has occurred, then the lungs will repair and clean themselves leading to normal health and life span. Women who smoke and take oral contraceptives are ten times more likely to suffer heart and circulatory diseases than non-smoking women. Passive smoking affects non-smokers who are at risk of developing smoking related diseases if in regular contact with tobacco smoke.

Legal Status

Selling any tobacco product to those under 16 is illegal and can result in a fine of up to £1000. There is no restriction on the possession and smoking of tobacco, though there are bans on most forms of public transport and in some public places. The commercial manufacture of tobacco requires a licence, but anyone can grow tobacco for their own use.

Sex and Drugs

All drugs will affect the user's judgement and probably reduce their inhibitions, increasing the likelihood that they may find themselves in situations they would normally avoid and which may be unsafe. Sexual situations may be more likely to occur when drugs are involved and it may be harder to remember the importance of practising safer sex when using drugs, thus increasing the risks of unplanned pregnancy and sexually transmitted infections (including HIV).

What To Do in an Emergency

Someone Is Unconscious But They Are Still Breathing And Their Heart Is Beating

Immediately dial 999 and call an ambulance, saying that you think alcohol or drugs might be involved. Put them into the recovery position on their side. If they are not breathing, check that their throat is not blocked; remove all foreign materials from their mouth. If they start breathing put them in the recovery position. If the heart is not beating and breathing has not started place them in the recovery position. Do not attempt basic life-support procedures (such as mouth-to-mouth resuscitation) unless you have been trained to do so.

Someone Has a Panic Attack

Be calm, reassure them, take them to a cool, quiet place and give them a few sips of water and nothing else. If there is no improvement in five to ten minutes call an ambulance.

Someone Becomes III After Dancing And May Have Taken Ecstasy

They may be experiencing heatstroke: they become very red and hot but do not sweat; they may feel sick and confused. Heatstroke can be very dangerous. Take them to a cool, quiet place and encourage them to slowly drink a non-fizzy soft drink. On no account give them coffee or any drinks that contain caffeine, as they will increase the effect of the drug. Call an ambulance. Keep them cool, by fanning them or pouring cool water over them until they reach normal body temperature. DO NOT let them become chilled – cover them if necessary.

Remember, when in doubt call an ambulance.

Calling an ambulance does not summon the police unless you say you need police assistance.

National Helplines

Release
0171 603 8654
Offers a 24-hour helpline providing advice on drug use and associated legal matters.

National Drugs Helpline
0800 776600
Offers a 24-hour service which gives advice about drugs and local services.

Regional Helplines

Avon and Somerset
0117 922 7997

East Midlands
Derby, Leicester and Nottingham
0115 924 0648

East and West Sussex
01273 722221

Essex
01245 353124

London
Brent, Ealing, Hammersmith and Fulham, Kensington and Chelsea and Westminster
0171 224 7229

London
Camden, Hackney, Haringey, Islington, Newham and Tower Hamlets
0171 837 7477

London
Greenwich, Lambeth, Lewisham, Southwark and Wandsworth
0171 378 1488

Merseyside
0151 236 4434

North
Bolton, Manchester, Rochdale, Salford and Stockport
0161 736 9540

Northern Ireland
Belfast: Health Promotion Branch, DHSS
01232 524234

Northumberland
Tyne and Wear
0191 233 1972

Scotland
Scottish Drugs Forum
Provides information on drugs services in Scotland.
0141 221 1175

Wales
Welsh Drug and Alcohol Unit
0122 667766

West Midlands
Birmingham, Dudley, Sandwell, Walsall and Wolverhampton
0121 553 5553

West Yorkshire
01274 741 274
If your area is not covered by one of these numbers, contact your local Health Promotion Unit.

We would like to thank Harvey Atkinson of the National Union of Students and the Student Union of the University of Brighton for allowing us to reproduce some of the material from the Student National Drugs Information Pack ('All Sorted').

8 *Food and Cooking*

Mum, how do you put the jacket on the potato?

Unless you have an interest in cooking, you probably won't have had to cook much for yourself until now. If you are in halls of residence some meals will be provided. If you find yourself in a student flat or house, however, you will have no option but to cook for yourself and, horror upon horrors, also budget and buy supplies. The other option, of course, is to live on takeaways – which is fine if you can afford it and you have good skin (but most students cannot afford it). In the appendix are some ideas for recipes popular with students. One of the most important ingredients for cheap grub is the seasoning – lots of herbs, spices and condiments to give flavour to cheap cuts and staples. First of all you need to check out what equipment you will need.

Equipping Yourself

In your flat or hall of residence you can expect to find the following kitchen equipment:

▩ fridge

▩ sink

▩ cooker

▩ kettle

▩ toaster

▓ microwave (maybe)

▓ basic pots and pans

▓ plates

▓ utensils.

It's a good idea to check it out first and then bring stuff a couple of weeks into term – otherwise you might find you have five microwaves and three kettles but no toaster.

When we'd settled into our flat after a few days, we realized we had five lemon squeezers and no frying-pan.

Cooking Equipment You Should Consider Buying For Yourself

Put identifying marks on your equipment to avoid end-of-year warfare.

Electrical (some of these might be provided)

▓ toaster

▓ kettle

▓ sandwich grill

▓ microwave

▓ hand mixer (for the more ambitious)

▓ food processor (for the very ambitious)

Other necessary equipment

▓ two or three sharp knives, various sizes

▓ grater

▓ chopping board and bread knife

▓ wooden spoon (new and clean)

▓ spatula

▓ wok

▓ non-stick frying-pan (not too expensive as it's bound to get ruined after three semesters of non-stop frying)

▓ ovenproof dish or large casserole pan able to go on the top of the stove and in the oven

▓ colander (big enough for draining pasta)

▓ mixing bowl, the bigger the better (2-litre is best)

▓ saucepan or two

▓ measuring jug

▓ vegetable peeler (but you can use a sharp knife)

▓ oven gloves

▓ tea towels (you can never have enough of these, but remember to wash occasionally – the tea towels, not you!)

▓ pepper-mill

▓ pan scrubber (your brother is not available)

▍ washing-up bowl (to keep your stuff in)

▍ can opener.

Crockery and cutlery

▍ cereal and soup bowls

▍ side plates

▍ dinner plates

▍ at least two knives

▍ at least two forks

▍ at least two spoons

▍ at least four teaspoons

▍ plastic food containers with lids, in various sizes that can fit inside each other

▍ labels (to label your tins and packets of food).

Sharing a flat will inevitably mean that cooking equipment becomes communal – expensive frying-pans will quickly become the permanent fry-up pan, scratched and covered with burnt-on food.

Also, the more stuff you have, the longer between washing-up sessions!

Much of this stuff can be picked up very cheaply. These things are unlikely to be a lifelong investment. Look at discount stores, second-hand shops, jumble sales and garage sales or get some old stuff from the family. Pans and things that were made a long time ago and have survived are better quality than a lot of gear on the market today, and you might be unwittingly making scrambled eggs in Einstein's old saucepan. Look out for glasses, mugs, teapot, storage jars, jugs, etc.

Starter Kit: Provisions

Basic Ingredients for Surviving the First Two Weeks

It's worth trying to slip these through with the family shopping.

- cereal

- emergency supply of long-life milk (half-litre size)

- butter or margarine

- vegetable oil (good enough for salad dressings)

- vinegar (cider or wine)

- flour

- salt and black pepper (preferably milled)

- coffee and tea

- sugar

- jams, marmalade, honey and peanut butter

- yeast extract (for the Marmite babies)

- tomato ketchup (one hogshead)

- mustard

- Worcestershire sauce

- stock cubes

- a selection of herbs and spices (see below)

- vegetarian stock powder or cubes (for veggies)

- cling film (non-PVC)

- aluminium foil

- cloths or sponges to wipe surfaces

- washing-up liquid

- black rubbish bags.

For the Culinary Artiste

If you enjoy cooking and are a keen and experienced cook, there are a few other items of equipment you might consider, although you yourself will probably be the best judge of what your requirements will be.

- scales

- measuring jug and spoons

- more pans

- sieve.

Definitely Not Required!

- rolling-pin (use a wine bottle)

- garlic press (chop finely or press to squeeze with a knife and salt)

- melon baller (don't bother)

- lemon zester (use a grater)

▓ asparagus boiler (use a deep-sided frying-pan instead and lay them flat)

▓ truffle oil.

A Cupboardful of Ingredients

OK, so now you have your basics.

From our research, it seems that most students eat a combination of Italian (pasta), Chinese (stir-fry) and Indian curried anything (especially vegetarians); so it might be a good idea to try to stock up on the ingredients for those cuisines as well. Choose the one you like – or all of them if you think you will cook a lot. It would be better to settle in for a few weeks before amassing a cupboardful of ingredients.

The Italian Job: Vital Ingredients

▓ oregano

▓ basil

▓ Parmesan cheese, ready grated (though fresh is better)

▓ olive oil

▓ pasta sauces

▓ dried pasta

▓ tomato purée

▓ garlic

▓ tinned tomatoes

Curry Flavour: Vital Ingredients

▓ dried or fresh chillies

▓ powdered ginger

▓ Cayenne pepper

▓ ground cumin

▓ ground coriander

▓ ground turmeric

▓ garam masala

▓ ghee (but you can use vegetable oil)

▓ rice

▓ garlic

▓ lentils

▓ split peas

▓ coconut cream.

Stir-crazy Cupboard: Vital Ingredients

▓ soy sauce

▓ fresh ginger (will last for several weeks in the fridge)

▓ vegetable oil

▓ sesame oil

▓ coriander

▓ chilli powder

▓ five-spice powder

▓ sugar

▓ garlic

▓ spring onions

▓ tinned bamboo shoots and water chestnuts

▓ cornflour (for thickening sauces).

There is also a good range of ready-made sauces available in the supermarkets for all sorts of different cuisines. These come in very handy when you need to make food fast.

Now you are ready – all you have to do is buy your fresh ingredients, depending on what you like to eat. Look for foods that are seasonal, locally grown or just on an unbelievable special offer and adjust your menu to suit.

A Healthy Diet

To stay healthy you need to eat a balanced diet. Basically this means combining the five main groups of valuable foods.

1. **Carbohydrates** Cereals and potatoes, pasta, rice. Should form a third of all the food eaten in a day. They provide energy, vitamins, minerals and fibre.

2. **Fruit and vegetables** You should eat at least five portions of fruit and veg a day, with meals or as snacks. They provide valuable vitamins, minerals and fibre.

3. **Milk and dairy foods** Yoghurt, cheese. These foods are rich in calcium, protein and B vitamins.

4. **Protein** Meat, fish, poultry, eggs, nuts, beans, chickpeas and lentils. They provide protein, vitamins and minerals.

5. **Foods containing fat and sugar** These foods are not essential to a healthy diet but add variety and interest. Some oil, especially olive oil, is extremely good for you and even a small amount of cakes and pastries can be part of a healthy diet as long as they aren't eaten in huge amounts.

Safe Cooking and Food Storage

Cooking can be a dangerous business. However, it is assumed, since you have made it to university, that you have some degree of nous. But if you've forgotten what you learnt at cookery classes at school, here's a reminder.

▓ Always wash your hands before you handle food.

▓ Never leave saucepan handles sticking out over the edge of the cooker where they can be knocked over.

▓ Never leave a frying-pan with fat or oil in it unattended.

▓ Have a fire-blanket handy near the cooker in case of fire. This or a fire extinguisher may well be provided.

▓ Try to avoid letting off the extinguisher after a good Saturday night at the rugby club. There are fines and a cost to pay for refilling them (£100 at Edinburgh University). And it's not much help if it's empty when the bacon and eggs set the kitchen on fire.

▓ Never cook wearing flammable clothes. The range of asbestos dungarees is limited due to concerns about asbestosis.

Don't Be Daunted by the Kitchen

Start by learning the basics and building up your knowledge and experience. After a while you will become more confident and perhaps more adventurous. It's rather like studying for your degree.

Food Hygiene

Not many students graduate with an Honours degree in food hygiene – stories of a failed chocolate mousse lurking in the deep recesses under the sink for three terms are not uncommon. A certain amount of care in looking after your provisions will save you unnecessary trips to the doctor suffering from botulism and in the long run will be an economy, as you won't be consigning mouldy green loaves to the local landfill.

Don't buy too much fresh food at any time. You will dislocate your shoulders staggering back from the supermarket and a dozen eggs will disappear in a midnight munchies session.

Fresh meat (if you touch the stuff)

Only buy enough for a couple of days and always keep it refrigerated. Don't take chances on this: if it smells bad, bin it. Bad meat can affect other food in the fridge as well. It should be stored uncovered on a plate on the bottom shelf of the fridge, so that if any blood drips off it does not contaminate other foodstuffs.

Frozen food

Handy to have if you trust the freezer section of the fridge. Generally only buy things that you can cook straight from frozen. Inevitably, if you remember to take out the chicken fillet in the morning to defrost and then your plans change, you will have to call the bomb-disposal unit to dispose of the radioactive mess three days later. Frozen fish is more practical as you can cook it from frozen and it's cheap. Most supermarket food labels carry information about freezing: how long and the star rating of the freezer. If you are going to freeze something fresh it should be done straightaway. Don't take frozen shopping to lectures.

Eggs

Can be stored out of the fridge in a cool place for a few days but it's better to keep them in the fridge. Raw eggs should be avoided – however desperate the hangover.

Fresh vegetables

Remove any plastic wrapping to stop them sweating.

Potatoes
Keep in a dark place (a cupboard or box).

Carrots
Keep in the fridge for five to six days.

Lettuce
Keep in vegetable crisper in bottom of the fridge.

Tomatoes
Can be kept on a window-sill for five to six days to retain a better flavour. Can become useful ammunition for dissident students confronting grant-cutting politicians.

Mushrooms
Keep in a bowl in the fridge for a week or so.

Bread

Best kept in a porous container like a wooden bread-bin. Even better toasted and eaten.

Canned foods

If you open a tin of food and only use half the contents, you should transfer the remainder to a bowl and cover with clingfilm before refrigeration. If this is a bit much, eat it all today and fast tomorrow.

Leftovers

If you have a dog (which you almost certainly won't) no problem. Otherwise, let the food cool down before putting it in a covered container and refrigerating. Contents of some student fridges have been shortlisted for the Turner Prize.

Dry goods

Keep in a dry warmish cupboard. Beware – that 10kg economy bag of porridge oats your mother pressed on you as you were struggling to get your surfboard on to the train may become a seething colony of weevils by your second year.

Pests (Apart from Your Flatmates)

Mice and cockroaches

Interesting to veterinary and biology students, but to others best avoided. Try to keep the floor and surfaces cleaned of food debris, store things properly and get rid of the rubbish regularly. Mice love chocolate.

> *I couldn't believe how gross I had become in just a few weeks – drinking out of dirty coffee mugs, even eating off the carpet. I soon reverted to home ways after we discovered mice droppings on the carpet.*

Flies

These little buzzers are not just a nuisance when that buzzing starts as you struggle to meet the essay deadline at four o'clock in the morning. They take a bite of food, regurgitate it back on to the remaining food and might lay a few eggs which will become writhing maggots if left to develop. Could be useful if you're keen on fishing, but generally avoided for reasons of cleanliness.

9 Looking After Yourself and Your Property

Someone's nicked my bike again.

Personal Safety

Safety must be thought about in all areas of university life. The physical environment, social environment and the students all play a part in making the university safe.

Here are some measures to consider. Some might seem obvious – but sometimes they are so obvious they can be overlooked.

Where You Live

▧ When choosing where you are going to live, try to ascertain what crime is like in that area. Visit the area at night and get a feel for the environment. Ask your fellow students where the danger zones are.

▧ Ensure that there is good street-lighting.

▧ If you live in an all-female flat, try to avoid needlessly telling people.

▧ Fit a chain to the front door and don't let strangers in. Make sure of the identity of people who come to read the meters, etc. If in doubt don't let them in – call the relevant head office.

▓ Change the locks with your landlord's permission – you don't know how many people have got keys (see page 154). Put a lock on your bedroom door.

▓ Being at university can cause bad feelings with people of the same age in the town. Don't antagonize them; avoid their haunts. (Male undergraduates are in more danger of being mugged).

▓ If you have arranged to meet someone who you do not know, such as a potential flatmate, meet on neutral territory where there are other people around, like the Union bar or a café.

▓ Avoid situations where you might be vulnerable. For instance, some of the laundry facilities at halls of residence are quite isolated and dark.

Rape

Rape is much more common than any of us know, because so many people never report it. If you become a victim, you will not only be physically hurt but also mentally. You must report the crime to the police. If you don't the perpetrator will inevitably do it again to someone else.

The police will also help you to find some counselling (such as a rape crisis centre).

Date Rape

University is a hothouse for sexual education and experimentation – if you want it. However, you may find yourself in a situation that you suddenly can't handle. Maybe you've had too much to drink, or you simply don't have the experience of how to judge what the other person wants. Date rape can be just one of these situations. Remember you always have a right to say 'no'.

> *I went to this fancy-dress party dressed as a fairy. I got completely hammered. The next morning I woke up in this bloke's bed. I still had my wings on but I couldn't remember a thing. Scary.*

Try to stay in control of the situation. If you feel yourself losing it stick with a friend who you can trust.

Travelling Alone

This is probably a more important issue for female students than male, although male students should also be aware of possible dangers. Men as well as women can be raped.

> *Five men were raped on the meadows at Edinburgh between 1996 and 1997 but no women. (Second-year female student at Edinburgh)*

▓ Never walk home alone at night through alleys, parks or woods – always travel with a friend. If that is impossible, spend the money to get a cab. Or, if possible, stay the night.

▓ Only use licensed taxis and minicabs. If you are a woman alone, many towns now have companies that provide minicabs driven by women for women. Or the uni may provide a transport system for journeys late at night. Some universities have an arrangement with a local taxi company that they will take you home even if you do not have any money, provided you give them your student card. They will return it to you when you pay the fare.

▓ Don't get into a railway carriage or compartment that is empty or has only one or two passengers.

▓ Sit near the driver on a bus if you are alone. If you are a woman on your own, sit near another woman.

▓ Carry a personal alarm – some Students' Unions issue these free to female students.

▓ Don't carry a weapon – it may be used against you.

▓ Take some lessons in self-defence – it is good for your self-confidence. (Contact police or your Students' Union for details).

> *I was with Tim the other day when we were mugged. He said he didn't have his wallet on him – so they demanded his personal stereo. I couldn't believe it – especially when he produced his wallet a few minutes later.*

If you find yourself in a situation where you are being mugged, it is best to cooperate. Hand over what they want, stay as calm as you can and leave the scene quietly. Afterwards you can report it to the police. This is preferable to having to file a report as you are having a knife pulled out of your chest in casualty. Muggers are dangerous, desperate and ruthless.

If you are a male student, you should be aware of all the above points – many of them are relevant to your own personal safety. Also, try to be mindful of how you handle yourself and how you can avoid putting women into situations where they might feel threatened.

▓ Don't follow a single female returning at night. Walk on the other side of the road.

▓ Walk a single female back to her accommodation late at night. If she doesn't invite you in for coffee, go home.

▓ Respect a woman's choice to say 'no' to sexual advances. (And you predatory females – try not to terrify the poor blokes into submission!)

▓ Don't leave your drink unattended in the bar. It might get spiked or someone might even drink it.

Sexual Harassment

As mentioned at the beginning of the book, university is a microcosm of the world. Unfortunately this also includes sexual harassment. Sexual harassment is unwanted, unwelcome, and unreciprocated, often deliberate, offensive and undermining.

If you feel that you are being harassed, you should report your feelings to the Student Welfare Officer. They will listen to your complaint seriously and sympathetically and try to resolve the situation.

Getting Around Safely

Bicycles

Bicycles are the universal means of transport at university. Unless you are a serious cyclist, take an inexpensive second-hand bike to uni with you. They have a habit of disappearing. This is reflected in the high cost of insuring them.

Ensure that you have adequate, strong enough locks. Lock the bicycle to something like a lamppost or a railing and make sure that the front wheel, which can easily be removed, is also locked to the frame. Never leave your bike unlocked and unattended, even for a minute. (So many saddles and wheels are stolen that people remove quick-release parts and carry them to lectures.)

It is strongly recommended that you wear a helmet (with the British Standard Kitemark). This offers some protection against head injury in case of an accident.

Bike sense

▌ Don't carry bags on the handlebars – have a rucksack, basket or pannier.

▌ Make sure that you have proper lights for night-time journeys (it can become dark at three in the afternoon in the middle of the winter in Inverness). Anyway, it's illegal not to have proper lights. You should remove them and take them with you when you park your bike or they will disappear in a flash.

▌ Don't leave a bicycle pump on the frame.

▌ Always make sure that your bicycle is in good working condition and safe to ride.

▌ A squirt of lubricating oil from time to time makes it much easier to cycle.

▓ Be careful when cycling in the rain – your brakes won't be so effective.

▓ Keep a record of your frame number. You will need this for insurance purposes.

▓ Assume all cars are driven by killer maniacs and all pedestrians are goats.

▓ Don't ride when you are legless – it's dangerous and it's also a criminal offence.

Cars

Most universities have quite strict regulations regarding students and cars. Unless you have some distance to travel, cars are not recommended as a means of transport for students for the following reasons.

▓ They are not green.

▓ They are highly expensive to run.

▓ They are a liability when you have to find somewhere to park.

▓ You won't get any exercise.

▓ You will be very popular amongst your friends on a rainy night.

However, if you do have a car, remember the following.

▓ You must have a driving licence, insurance, tax and a valid MOT certificate.

▓ With petrol, tax, insurance and maintenance, it can cost more than £1000 per year to run even the most basic rollerskate.

▓ When giving people lifts, you can ask them to contribute towards the petrol. This is particularly useful at the beginning or end of term if you have a long distance to cover.

▓ Don't overload the car with either people or possessions. There is a maximum to the number of people that you can carry in any specific model.

▓ Be aware of cyclists. Assume they are irresponsible baboons on two wheels.

▓ Leave the car well alone during Freshers' Week. It will probably take you until week four before you can pass a breathalyser test.

All this may sound rather negative. If you are responsible, can afford a car and it's OK with the authorities, cars can be a safe form of transport, especially for single women travelling late at night. But do not give strangers a lift, even if you've just met them at a party, unless you have some other friends in the car with you. And keep the doors locked when travelling alone.

Motor-bikes and Scooters

▓ You need to have the same documentation as a motorist: licence, tax, insurance, registration and MOT.

▓ Make sure that you have the right equipment to wear. Your helmet should be unmarked and undamaged. If it is dropped, it could become ineffective in a prang. Have good boots and gloves and ideally leather or tough PVC trousers and jacket. Reflective material is good – that's why the police use it.

▓ Maintain your machine well.

▓ Be a little paranoid. Assume everyone else on the street is out to get you. That's if they can see you – you are probably invisible to them.

In-line and Rollerskates

Becoming more popular as a way of getting around, although you might pong a bit during lectures.

▓ Knee and elbow pads and a helmet are recommended. Be thoughtful of pedestrians and try to avoid terrorizing grannies.

▓ Assume everyone else got stuck somewhere back in the mid-80s.

Pogo Stick or Stilts

▓ Original but useless, really.

▓ Assume nothing – you're bonkers.

Skateboard

▓ Permanently adolescent surfer dude victim. Sad.

Personal Property

After you have recovered from your Marxist phase and finished reading Pierre Joseph Proudhon's *Qu'est que la propriete*? you will suddenly discover that you are in fact still a materialistic pig. This will first be noticed when your milk disappears from the communal fridge.

Protecting Your Property

One of the problems, especially if you are sharing a flat, is that you have to rely on everyone else doing their bit.

> *Barnie used to leave his front door open all the time until someone walked in and nicked his expensive stereo. He was asleep in the next room at the time.*

▓ You should always make sure the doors and windows are locked when you are all out and also lock your bedroom if you can (especially in the summer). Some insurance companies insist that you have a deadlock on your bedroom door to validate the policy.

- Draw the curtains at night and when you are all out during the day, so passers-by can't case the joint.

- Avoid bringing your £23,000 Rolex Oyster and other valuable possessions with you to university. It will be a hotbed of petty pilfering and, unfortunately, more serious crime.

- Don't conceal keys outside the flat. However creative you might think you are, a professional burglar will be even more imaginative.

- Don't leave expensive possessions at university during the vacation. Many thefts happen when not many people are around.

Insurance

Some insurance companies offer special deals for students. The best advice is to shop around before deciding. It is also worth checking whether or not your possessions are already covered under your parents' policy. The size of the premium will depend on the area you live in and the amount for which you are insured. It is also cheaper if you are in a hall of residence.

Possessions insurance

This policy would generally cover all your possessions – with some exclusions, such as a computer – against theft, damage and loss. You may need to specify certain more valuable items such as cameras and a hi-fi and to provide proof of purchase, such as a receipt. Check whether you are covered in the vacation and when your property is in transit.

Computer insurance

The premium on this sort of policy is worked out as a percentage of the value of the equipment – usually between three and ten per cent.

Bicycle insurance

Again a specific insurance relating to the value of your bike. It may include a sum for injury in an accident.

General Advice On All Insurance Policies

Make sure you read all the small print on the policy. There may be all sorts of exclusions, such as whether the property is occupied during vacations, and there may be stipulations regarding goods above a certain value. There will also be stipulations about what sort of security you need to have and how you use it.

> *I knew these guys who always left their back door open. Then they were burgled. So they had to lock the back door and break it. Unfortunately they did it from the inside and the police report stated that the burglars broke out through the back door.*

Also, there is usually an excess. An excess is a sum of money that you have to pay towards any claim. For example, if the excess is £25 it's not worth claiming for a radio that is only worth £20.

Insurance companies can be very slow at making a payment to you and it might be several weeks or months before everything is sorted out and settled. It is worth asking if they have any guarantee of swift payment. If they don't, you may not be able to stump up for a new bike and walking three miles to lectures every day can become very tedious.

Remember, if you are having problems with your insurance company, you can always consult the Insurance Ombudsman. They will let you know if you are being treated fairly and if not may bring pressure on to the company.

10 Where Next? CVs and Job-hunting

I'm doing an internship in the holidays at the company I want to work for when I graduate – it's a good way to see if I like it and make a good impression.

One of the most important reasons for entering higher education is to prepare you for the job market. Part of the argument for the introduction of tuition fees is that, as a graduate, you will have expectations of a higher earning capacity. But how do you set about finding a job?

Careers Advice

The institution at which you are studying should have a Careers Service and this should be your first port of call. It's a good idea to speak to them some time before you complete your degree – ideally in your second year. Then you will have plenty of time to get some work experience in the vacation.

They will be able to assess you, your interests and your qualifications (all being well) and help you to decide in which direction you might wish to pursue a career. This can be particularly useful if you are studying a non-vocational degree with what may seem to you little relevance in the outside world.

There will be listings of potential employers and opportunities and they may be able to arrange interviews for you. There will also be information about future milk rounds.

The Careers Service may also arrange lectures and seminars to help you to understand your future in the world of employment. Use the Careers Service and liaise with them in your penultimate year. Don't forget it's free and they have good contacts.

Where To Look for Jobs

Milk Rounds

Milk rounds are when companies send recruitment officers to universities to look for potential candidates to employ in the future. It is worth keeping an eye on who is coming as this can be a very useful short cut.

Job Fairs

The university may also arrange a Job Fair. This is not unlike the Fresher's Fair, but rather than offering you the opportunity to join the 'Custard Appreciation Society' you will be obtaining real serious information from the 'grown-up' world.

Networking

Networking is a fact of life and you should not feel ashamed to network. Talk to friends and family who may have opportunities or contacts in the line of business that interests you. It's much easier to get your foot in the door if you have a personal introduction. More often than not people are very willing to try and help you, especially if you appear enthusiastic in your intentions. Other people with whom you might network are the lecturers and tutors on your course. This is more likely to be relevant if your course is vocational, as they will certainly have a number of professional contacts.

The Press

Check the local and national newspapers which will carry listings of opportunities for graduates. Most national broadsheets have ads for different areas of the job market on different days. Find out which day is relevant to you and check the listings regularly. There are also specialist publications for different professions. For example, in the advertising profession there is *Campaign*, amongst many others.

Internet

Use the web to check out any job opportunities. By this time you should be completely *au fait* with how to do it.

CV (Curriculum Vitae)

When you start the process of job searching you should prepare your CV so that it is ready for when you need it.

A CV is the story of your life so far – a brief summary that a future employer can glance through to make a quick assessment. It should contain the following information:

- your full name

- your age

- where you can be contacted (if for example you travel away from the university during the vacations there should be more than one address and the relevant dates when you will be at each address)

- telephone contact number

- a short personal profile of yourself and your ambitions

- details of your secondary education

    - name of school and address
    - GCSE qualifications (subjects and grades)
    - A-level qualifications (subjects and grades)
    - other exam certificates held

Figure 10.1: Sample CV

CURRICULUM VITAE

NAME: Laura Mayfield

ADDRESS: 46 Clifton Hill, Headingford, Manchester
                  LS4 1FW

TELEPHONE: 0116 415 5789

DATE OF BIRTH: 27 July 1978

NATIONALITY: British

EDUCATION:

1988–96	Whitefields Comprehensive School, Whitefields, Manchester.	8 GCSE's including Maths and English (five at grade A). 3 A-levels in French, Maths and History (BBC).
1996 to date	University of Manchester	BA European Studies with Politics (2:1 average, graduating 1999)

WORK EXPERIENCE:

August 1997 (two-weeks)	*European Business News* – 10 Fleet Place, London, EC4M 7RB	Office junior
October 1997 to date	'The Manchester Student' Newspaper – Manchester Metropolitan University Union.	Reporter
January 1998 to date	Part-time work at the River Café – Old Trafford, Manchester.	

VOLUNTARY WORK:
A committed member of International Voluntary Service since July 1997. Attended a work camp in Madrid, preparing for 'Second Encounter for Humanity and Against Neo-Liberalism'.

OTHER SKILLS:
I can use a computer and am familiar with several wordprocessing packages. Full clean driving licence.

INTERESTS:
Music, cinema, art, theatre.

ADDITIONAL INFORMATION:
I am a hardworking, innovative, confident, positive individual with an enquiring mind. Have been asked to be editor of the Political page of 'The Machester Student' next year. Also was elected to represent Manchester University at NUS Conference 1997.

REFEREES:
James McGrath
Financial Times
Southwark Bridge Road
London, SE1 IHL.
Tel: 0171 773 5000

Belinda Summers
Manageress of River Café
Old Trafford
Manchester.
Tel: 0161 789 4352

▌ details of higher education

  - name of the institution
  - degree course studied and (expected) classification
  - any intermediate results

▌ any other relevant skills or qualifications, eg driving licence, computer literacy

▌ brief details of any work experience

▌ details of any other jobs that you have had

▌ a few interests outside work

▌ personal references (names and addresses of people who are willing to act as referees, eg former employer or manager of your hockey team).

Your CV is a very important document and you should take time over preparing it. It may receive a 30-second glance from an employer, so it must create a good and clear impression. Your career service will help you prepare it. It should be not more than two pages long, clearly presented, set out on a word processor on good quality paper and always up to date. Don't leave blank spaces in your life. If you took a gap year, briefly put some information about this between secondary education and higher education. It may make you sound independent, pioneering and interesting, even if you spent the winter snowboarding and the summer surfing. Dress it up with details of how you financed it, or perhaps the fact that you were teaching your hobby – all sorts of different things catch an employer's eye.

Letter of Application

If you see an advertisement or hear of an opening that interests you, write a letter of application immediately. As with your CV, it should be well-presented, to the point and politely formal.

What You Should Write

▓ name, address and telephone number

▓ name and address of the company to which you are applying (check the spelling carefully)

▓ the date of your letter

▓ the publication and date on which you saw the advertisement

▓ any reference number you may have been asked to quote

▓ why the position interests you

▓ a brief summary of what you may offer to the company

▓ a request for an interview or an application form.

Read the advertisement carefully: it may ask for your application to be handwritten, in which case you don't want to word process it! They may request that you send a CV or positively tell you not to send one. Make sure you provide what is required.

Keep a copy of your letter and the advertisement. If you are sent for an interview it will refresh your memory as to what you have said.

Telephone Application

The advertisement that you have seen may ask you to telephone in response, perhaps to request an interview or an application form.

You need to be composed and have all the relevant information to hand. If you have to use a payphone use a phonecard or make sure that you have plenty of change. Some companies may keep you hanging on as they bounce you around the switchboard.

▓ Read the advertisement carefully.

Figure 10.2: Sample letter

15b Grafton Hall
Grafton Road
Glasgow
0141 427 3542

17 April 2000

Personnel Manager
Acorn Broadcasting
Acorn House
Birmingham BJ4 9QT

Dear Sir/Madam

Ref: TDC 6300 8

I am writing in response to an advertisement in the *Broadcasting Broadsheet* on 12 April. I would like to apply for the position as 'Trainee Assistant Production Manager'. I enclose my CV as requested.

I am currently in my final year of Media Studies at Pollockshields University. My final paper, which I am preparing at the moment, covers the subject: 'The Effects of Australian Soap Operas on Teenage Diet'.

As you will see from my CV, I have gained valuable work experience at a number of broadcasting houses during my time at university.

I feel that I would be a very suitable candidate for this position. I have demonstrated my management skills in three university productions, the last of which won a prize at the Edinburgh Festival.

I hope that you will consider my application and I look forward to hearing from you to arrange a meeting.

Yours faithfully,

Arnold Grove
Enc.

▓ Note the name of the person or department that you need to speak to.

▓ Note the date of the application.

▓ Note down the job description.

▓ Prepare a short statement of why they should be interested in you.

▓ Have your CV in front of you.

When you call, ask for the relevant person or department. If it's a department, listen carefully to the name of the person to whom you are speaking and write it down. Introduce yourself clearly and politely, saying which position interests you. Don't speak too fast and don't say too much.

For example: 'Good morning, my name is Sheila Bowie. I'm calling with reference to the advertisement in the *Circus Post* for the job as trainee lion tamer.'

Pay attention to the questions you are asked and answer them accurately, briefly and to the point. The person you are talking to may wish to contact you by telephone again. If this is not possible, arrange a time to call back, at her convenience, and stick to it. At the end of a conversation, thank her for the time she has spent talking to you, using her name. If she hasn't offered you an interview, suggest that you would be available to meet her in person and say goodbye politely.

For example: 'Thank you very much for your time, Mrs. Plunkett. It was very interesting talking to you; the sequinned costume sounds very exciting. Could you send me an application form, or if you prefer I would be happy to come and see you. Thank you again. Goodbye.'

Application Forms

If you are sent an application form to fill out for a job, you must be careful with it. Don't leave it on a chair, where your flatmates might sit on it, or in the kitchen to get splattered with tomato ketchup or coffee stains.

First of all you should read it through very carefully, taking a note of any instructions about filling it in (eg BLOCK CAPITALS, etc).

Make a photocopy and fill this in first. This is especially important if you have to write a personal profile or reasons for being considered. Run these profiles past your flatmates or ask for the opinion of the Careers Office.

When you are happy with the photocopied version, you can fill in the real thing. Do this carefully and neatly, avoiding mistakes.

Make sure that you fill in all the questions that are asked, leaving no blanks. If any sections do not apply to you, write n/a (not applicable).

This application form should be completed promptly, within a couple of days of receiving it. When you have completed it, check it through for any mistakes and make a further photocopy. This will be an important reference document should you be called for an interview.

Send it back to the company by first class post; this shows a positive intent.

Follow-up and Hassling

If, after a reasonable amount of time, you have had no response to a letter or an application form, it is worth chasing it up. It may have got lost. At worst, you will just be bringing your name to their attention again.

Write a polite covering letter and staple it to a copy of your previous correspondence.

Interviews

You may be asked to go for an interview. Read the invitation carefully, to see exactly what is required from you. The interview could take several forms. You might be grilled by a panel in an intimidatory format, or it may be a less formal one-to-one interview. Alternatively, you may be interviewed as part of a group of candidates or the company may organize a residential weekend which will involve social events as well as assignments.

Figure 10.3: Sample follow-up letter

15b Grafton Hall
Grafton Road
Glasgow
0141 427 3542

6 May 2000

Personnel Manager
Acorn Broadcasting
Acorn House
Birmingham BJ4 9QT

Dear Sir/Madam

Ref: TDC 6300 8

I am writing with reference to my letter dated April 17 2000. As I have not heard from you, I am enclosing a copy of the letter and also a copy of my CV.

If my letter has been lost, I hope that I am not too late to be considered for the position.

I look forward to hearing from you in the near future.

Yours faithfully,

Arnold Grove
Enc.

Preparation

▓ Decide how you plan to travel, find out timetables and allow plenty of time.

▓ Find out information on the company – including reading any bumph they have sent to you.

▓ If you are very nervous, organize a mock interview with the Careers Service.

▓ Decide what you are going to wear and ensure it is clean and ready. (Don't look too provocative, boys!)

▓ Assess exactly what the position being offered involves.

▓ Decide why you are the person for the job.

▓ Draw up a list of questions that you anticipate you will be asked. Prepare answers. You may be asked to list your weaknesses as well as your strengths.

▓ Draw up a list of questions that you can ask if you have the opportunity.

▓ Ensure you have copies of any correspondence: forms, CVs, etc.

▓ Think of other things that may interest a prospective employer.

Going for the Interview

▓ Don't worry if you arrive too soon. Use the time to run over your prepared answers and questions and refresh your mind on the nature of the job.

▓ Try to be relaxed and sharp. (Don't go partying the night before and turn up with a Force 10 hangover.)

▓ When you are summoned, knock on the door before entering.

▓ Expect to be introduced and be prepared to shake hands.

▓ When you are offered a seat, sit comfortably but don't slouch. Avoid crossing arms or legs.

▓ When you are asked a question, address the speaker directly and look him or her in the face.

▓ Pause before answering to decide what you are planning to say.

▓ Make your answers precise and avoid excessive wit. A small amount of levity can reduce tension, but you need to assess the mood before trying it.

▓ Don't waffle.

▓ Show enthusiasm.

▓ Don't smoke.

▓ If you are unclear about anything, ask the speaker to repeat the question.

▓ Be polite and avoid using any bad language.

▓ Be ready to ask questions if given the opportunity, but don't ask too many.

▓ At the end of the interview, be grateful and shake hands before saying goodbye.

▓ Don't trip over your briefcase on the way out.

▓ Don't leave your sandwiches behind.

▓ If you are at a residential interview, don't get pissed in the bar.

▓ Be keen to be involved in any tasks that you may be set.

▓ In a group interview avoid either dominating the discussion or not saying anything at all.

When the interview draws to a close, you will probably be informed when you can expect to hear if you have been successful. Don't presume to ask at this stage about company pensions, perks, pay, etc. You will have plenty of time to do that later.

If you decide to go to the pub afterwards, leave the area first. A prospective employer may not be impressed if they bump into you in the 'Black Goat' 20 minutes after your interview.

So there it is.

GOOD LUCK!

Appendix
Basic Student Meals

Potatoes

Potatoes can be baked in their jackets, fried, sautéed and mashed. They can be eaten alone, or used as a topping for a pie or as a container for other ingredients. They are cheap, nutritious and filling. Potatoes are an excellent provider of carbohydrate, one of the important food groups.

One of the most popular dishes that appeared on our student survey was the ubiquitous baked potato. And by the way the jacket comes with it, in case you didn't know!

How To Bake Potatoes in their Jacket

You can cook potatoes in the microwave if you have one – that way you will speed up the cooking time considerably but you won't have a nice crispy, crunchy skin that you will have if you bake them in the oven. The best way is to combine the two methods. It's much quicker, saves electricity and you get the crispy skin.

Microwave only

Wash the potato, pierce with a fork and wrap in kitchen towel. Microwave on high (700 W) for 8 minutes for a medium-sized potato.

Oven only

Cooking time: about 45 minutes.
Wash, pierce and bake in a moderate oven at 200C/400F Gas Mark 6 for 1 hour.

To speed things up you could pierce the potato with a metal fork and leave it in whilst it cooks. It helps to cook the centre of the potato but make sure you don't grip the fork when you take it out – it will be baked as well.

Microwave and oven

Preheat oven to 230C/450F. Wash and pierce the potato. Microwave on high for 6 minutes (700W), transfer to oven and cook for 15 minutes until crispy.

Ideas for fillings

- butter and salt
- cottage cheese/bacon
- any other cheese: Cheddar, mozzarella, Boursin
- tomato sauce, vegetables and topped with cheese (a pizza potato)
- ham
- sour cream and chives
- baked beans
- tuna fish
- fried egg
- creamed spinach
- pesto sauce.

Balance the meal with a salad.

Other Ideas for Potatoes

Rosti (Swiss grated potato cake)

Feeds 4.
Preparation time: 20 minutes.
Cooking time: 15 minutes.
You will need:

- 750g/1.5lb potatoes, unpeeled
- salt and pepper
- 1 tablespoon oil
- 25g/1oz butter.

1. All you do is boil the potatoes whole for 10 minutes. Drain, cool, peel and coarsely grate then season with salt and pepper.
2. Heat the oil and the butter together in a medium-sized frying-pan. Spoon in the potatoes, pressing them down with the spatula, so they are all one level. Fry for 10 minutes, brown top under the grill, then serve in wedges.

Variations

Add onions, cheese, other vegetables, bacon, ham and herbs. Excellent with fried eggs.

Mash

Real comfort food. There is nothing quite so comforting as fluffy mashed potatoes. You need to use the right variety of potato – floury – to achieve success; Maris Piper or King Edward are the most common.

Feeds 4–6.
Preparation time: 5 minutes.
Cooking time: 20 minutes.
You will need:

- 1kg/2.2lbs potatoes, peeled
- salt and pepper
- 75g/3fl oz milk (plus a little cream)
- 25g/1oz butter or margarine.

1. Boil the potatoes until tender. This will take about 20 minutes.
2. Mash whilst still hot with a potato masher (or fork) then place over a low heat and add hot milk, season with lots of pepper and salt and add a knob of butter.

Variations

Add crushed garlic to the mash, cook half parsnip (or turnip) and half potato, or cook half sweet potato and half regular potato.

Rice

Rice is a fantastic staple to have in the cupboard, once you have mastered how to cook it you can make lots of different dishes. Many people have problems with rice but basically if you read the instructions on the packet you should be fine. Easy-cook rice is hard to ruin, brown rice takes longer to cook than white, long-grain rice can be tricky but not if you follow the instructions and risotto rice needs lots of liquid and should be sticky at the end.

Cooking Long-grain Rice

Feeds 6.
Preparation time: 5 minutes.
Cooking time: about 15 minutes.
You will need:

- 1 tablespoon oil
- 1 garlic clove, crushed
- 350g/12oz dry rice
- boiling water.

1. Rinse the rice in running water until the water runs clear. Use a sieve.
2. Heat the oil in a medium-sized saucepan, add the garlic and fry gently over low heat for 2 minutes. Add the rice and stir over heat for a minute.
3. Pour boiling water over until there is the same amount above the rice as the depth of the rice itself.
4. Bring back to the boil. Cover the pan, reduce the heat and simmer for 10–15 minutes. When you remove the lid, all the water should have been absorbed and the rice will be cooked.

Hints and Tips for Rice

If the water has boiled dry but the rice is still a little crunchy, add a little more water and cook for a few more minutes. If it is a bit mushy, drain it, rinse under cold water and then dry it off in a roasting tin in a medium oven for 15 minutes.

Cook's tip

Rice is an excellent ingredient for stretching a meal if some mates turn up unexpectedly. Especially good for curry nights as you can turn your curry into a Biryani by just adding more rice and stirring it all together.

Other Recipes for Rice

Rice pilaff

A rice pilaff is rice enriched with oil or butter and cooked slowly until the stock or water has been absorbed (a bit like the above); but then you can stir in other ingredients and make a one pot meal.

Feeds 4.
Preparation time: 45 minutes.
Cooking time: about 20 minutes.
You will need:

- 250g/8oz long grain rice
- 25g/1oz butter plus 1 tablespoon
- 1 tablespoon oil
- 1 onion, chopped
- 100g/4oz peas
- 100g/4oz mushrooms, sliced
- 100g/4oz sweetcorn, drained
- 300–360ml/10–12fl oz chicken/vegetable stock
- salt and freshly ground black pepper

1. Soak the rice for 30 minutes while you prepare the remaining ingredients. Drain, then melt half the butter with the oil in a medium-sized saucepan. Add the onion and fry for 5 minutes.
2. Stir in the rice and cook for a further 2 minutes. Pour over the stock and bring to the boil. Cover the pan, reduce the heat to low and cook for 15–20 minutes, or until the liquid is absorbed.
3. In a small pan, melt the remaining butter and cook the mushrooms for a couple of minutes, then add to the rice, together with the peas and sweetcorn. Season with salt and pepper and serve.

Risotto

A risotto is a creamy, delicious dish and to be authentic you should really use short-grain Italian Arborio rice. The creaminess is achieved by adding small amounts of stock during the process.

Feeds 4.
Preparation time: 5 minutes.
Cooking time: 30 minutes.
You will need:

- 75g/3oz butter
- 1 tablespoon olive oil
- 1 medium-sized onion, finely chopped
- 375g/12oz Arborio (risotto) rice
- 1–1.2l (2–2.5 pints) chicken/vegetable stock
- 100g/4oz coarsely grated Parmesan cheese

1. Melt 50g/2oz of the butter together with the oil in a large saucepan over medium heat. Add the onion and fry for 5 minutes, until golden.
2. Stir in the rice and cook for 2 minutes, then pour in a ladleful of hot stock and keep stirring until the liquid has been absorbed. Continue adding the stock a little at a time, until the rice is cooked but still firm. It will take about 20–25 minutes and you must stir it continuously.
3. Stir in the remaining butter, season with salt and pepper and serve hot with Parmesan.

Variations

You can add lots of different ingredients at the end – it is the perfect dish for vegetarians. Sautéed courgettes and mushrooms are particularly good.

Pasta

Pasta is quick to make, healthy and cheap. It's real store-cupboard food that you can knock up without having to rush out and buy lots of fresh ingredients. Fresh garlic is recommended though. You generally allow 100g/4oz dried spaghetti per person. Of course you could always buy ready-prepared tomato sauce but home-made tomato sauce is cheaper.

Pasta and Tomato Sauce

Feeds 4.
Preparation time: 5 minutes.
Cooking time: 25 minutes.
You will need:

* 1 packet 450g/1lb dried spaghetti
* pinch of salt

For the tomato sauce:

* 2 tablespoons olive oil (or vegetable oil)
* 1 large onion, peeled and finely chopped
* 2 garlic cloves, crushed
* 2 x 325g/14oz value tins of tomatoes, chopped
* 2 tablespoons tomato puree
* 1 teaspoon dried oregano
* 1 teaspoon sugar (makes the tomatoes less acidic)
* half teaspoon salt
* freshly ground black pepper.

1. First make the tomato sauce: heat the oil in a saucepan. Add the onion and fry over medium heat for 5–7 minutes, until the onion is soft and translucent but not brown. Add the garlic and cook for a further 2 minutes.
2. Stir in the tomatoes, tomato purée, oregano, sugar, salt and black pepper. Bring to the boil. Lower the heat and simmer over low heat for about 15 minutes, stirring from time to time.
3. Meanwhile, bring a large pan of lightly salted water to a rolling boil. You can add a few drops of olive oil to the water. (The secret to successful pasta is to use a big pan and lots of water.) Hold the spaghetti in the water and it will soon soften and slide into the pan. Stir it around a few times to separate the strands. Cook for 8–10 minutes until it is just done. (The Italians eat it – Al dente – which means 'with a bite'). Strain and return to the pan and add a few drops of olive oil. Serve with the tomato sauce straightaway.

Spaghetti

* If you find that the spaghetti is over-cooked, drain off the hot water and quickly rinse it under some cold water to stop the cooking process – the same applies to rice, by the way.

Making the Most of Tomato Sauce

▓ You can mix lots of other things with the tomato sauce, such as bacon, minced meat, chicken, mushrooms and peppers.

▓ If you have any left over, it keeps for about a week in a screw-top jar in the fridge; or you can freeze it.

▓ This tomato sauce can also be used as a topping for pizza and the base for minestrone soup, chilli con carne or salsa.

Some other quick pasta sauces:

▓ cooked broccoli, garlic, chilli and anchovy (anchovy can be omitted as it is quite expensive)

▓ gently fried onions, garlic, aubergine and chilli

▓ gently fried onions, tuna fish and cheese

▓ gently fried onions, garlic, mushrooms and cream.

Vegetarian Lasagne

The great thing about this lasagne is that it is really healthy as you use cottage cheese which should be lumpy instead of white sauce, which usually is lumpy and shouldn't be. This will keep for several days in the fridge and can also be eaten cold.

Feeds 6
Preparation time: 30 minutes.
Cooking time: 1 hour.
You will need:

▓ 2 tablespoons olive or vegetable oil

▓ a selection of vegetables including 1 onion, 2 cloves of garlic, 1 aubergine, cubed, 2 peppers, cubed, two 325g/14oz tinned tomatoes, chopped, plus courgettes, leeks, potatoes (all cubed) or any other vegetables you have laying around

▓ salt and freshly ground black pepper

▓ half teaspoon dried oregano

▓ half teaspoon dried basil

▓ 1 packet no-cook lasagne

▓ 2 large tubs value cottage cheese

▓ 100g/4oz Cheddar cheese or other, grated

1. First of all make a vegetable stew: heat the oil in a large saucepan, fry the onion and garlic for 5 minutes, then add all the other vegetables, season with salt and pepper and the herbs. Cook for 30 minutes, stirring from time to time.
2. Heat the oven to 350F/180C/Gas Mark 4. Using an ovenproof dish make layers of vegetables, lasagne, cottage cheese, vegetables, etc until all the ingredients are used up. Top with a layer of grated cheese.
3. Bake in the oven for 1 hour.

Bolognese

If you eat beef, one of the easiest and most versatile recipes is cooked minced beef – you can turn it into so many dishes by adding seasoning. If you don't eat beef, you can substitute it with TVP/TSP (textured vegetable protein/textured soya protein).

Basic bolognese

Feeds 4.
Preparation time: 5 minutes.
Cooking time: 45 minutes.
You will need:

- 2 tablespoons vegetable oil
- 1 onion, chopped
- 2 cloves of garlic, chopped (optional)
- 450g/1lb minced beef
- 1 teaspoon sugar
- 1 teaspoon oregano or basil
- salt and black pepper
- 245g/14oz tinned tomatoes.

1. Heat the oil in a saucepan, add the onion and garlic and fry over low heat for 5 minutes. Stir in the meat and cook for a further 5 minutes.
2. Season the mixture with the herbs, salt, pepper and sugar and stir in the tomatoes.
3. Bring to the boil, reduce the heat to low and simmer for about 30–35 minutes, stirring from time to time.

Cook's tip

Bolognese can also be used as a basis for Shepherd's pie or chilli con carne – see below.

Variations

Shepherd's pie
Feeds 4

- Bolognese sauce (p179)
- 2 carrots, sliced
- 2 celery stalks, sliced
- 1 tablespoon of Worcestershire sauce
- 1 teaspoon thyme
- 1 tablespoon gravy granules
- 120ml/4fl oz water
- 1 kg/2.2lb mashed potato (see page 173)

Mix the other ingredients into the basic Bolognese sauce, spoon into an ovenproof dish, cover with potato and bake in a medium oven for 30 minutes.

Chilli con carne
Feeds 4
You will need:

- Bolognese sauce (p179)
- 1–2 teaspoons paprika
- 1 tablespoon cumin seeds
- half–1 teaspoon hot chilli powder
- 1–2 tins of red kidney beans.

Add all the extra ingredients to the basic Bolognese and cook for a further 30 minutes. Serve with rice or baked potatoes (or more if you want to stretch it).

Quick and Easy Chinese Wokkery

A wok is one of the most useful items you can have in your kitchen. It can be used to stir-fry, deep fry, boil, shallow fry, make curries in and even boil pasta.

If you buy a new wok and it is not non-stick it will need to be seasoned.

Seasoning a Wok

Scrub the wok with some hot soapy water to remove any machine grease. Rinse it off, dry it and place it over a low flame. Add 1 tablespoon of vegetable oil and rub this all over the inside using a some kitchen paper. Heat it for another 10 minutes and then remove from the heat. Wipe the inside and then repeat the process. Thereafter you should only ever wipe your wok clean with damp kitchen paper after using it and rub in more oil.

Stir-fried Chicken

Feeds 2–4.
Preparation time: 10 minutes.
Cooking time: 10 minutes.
Can be eaten cold the next day.
You will need:

- 4 tablespoons vegetable oil
- 1 egg, beaten
- 225g/8oz chicken flesh cut into strips (thighs are cheap)
- 2 cloves of garlic, crushed
- 2.5cm/1in piece of fresh root ginger, peeled and finely chopped
- 60ml/2fl oz tablespoons chicken stock (made with about a quarter of a stock cube crumbled into some boiling water)
- 1 tablespoon soy sauce
- 2 spring onions, finely sliced
- 100g/4oz bean sprouts – you can grow these from mung beans
- 100g/4oz Chinese or ordinary green cabbage
- salt and ground black pepper.

1. Put the wok on the cooker for a few seconds before you add the oil. Pour in the oil and allow it to heat then add the egg and swirl it around to cook into a thin omelette. Lift out and cut into thin ribbons. Set aside.
2. Add the strips of chicken and stir-fry until golden brown. Remove and set aside.
3. Add the garlic and ginger and stir-fry for 30 seconds. Pour in the stock and soy sauce and bring to the boil.
4. Stir in the spring onion and a few seconds later the cabbage. Stir-fry for about 3 minutes, until just tender, then add the bean sprouts, chicken and egg. Season with salt and pepper.

Stir-fried Vegetables with Noodles

Feeds 4–6.
Preparation time: 10 minutes.
Cooking time: 10 minutes.
You will need:

- 250g/8oz packet of egg noodles
- 3 tablespoons vegetable oil
- 2 garlic cloves, chopped
- 4 spring onions, sliced
- 2.5cm/1in length of fresh ginger, peeled and finely sliced or chopped
- 2 carrots, cut into sticks
- 2 celery stalks cut into sticks
- 30ml/2fl oz light soy sauce
- 1 tsp. sesame oil
- 120ml/5fl oz chicken or vegetable stock
- 1 green or red pepper, cut in half, deseeded then cut into sticks
- quarter cabbage cut into shreds
- 250g/8oz bean sprouts, washed and drained

1. Soak the egg noodles in boiling water for 7 minutes until soft. Rinse under cold water then drain and place in a bowl. Mix in a little sesame oil to stop them sticking together.
2. Heat the wok, add the vegetable oil and heat for a few second then add the garlic, spring onion and ginger.
3. Holding the wok firmly with one hand, stir-fry the ingredients for 1 minute, tossing them in the pan with a long spoon or spatula.
4. Add the carrots and celery. Stir-fry for a further 5 minutes before adding half the soy sauce, oil and stock.
5. Stir in the pepper, cabbage and bean sprouts and continue stir-frying for another 5 minutes.
6. Finally stir in the noodles and the remaining soy sauce, oil and stock. Cook until heated through. Taste and adjust the seasoning, adding more soy sauce if desired.

Note: You can use other vegetables like French beans, mushrooms and leeks – any vegetable you like. See what you can use up and what is cheap. This dish also tastes great cold.

Curry

Curry becomes compulsory once you go to university. Even the most hardened curry-haters tend to give in after their first year and even start to enjoy it after the second.

Nowadays you can buy very good ready-made sauces and spice mixtures but once you gain a little confidence it's fun experimenting with your own spices.

Chicken Tikka

Chicken tikka is not so much a curry but more spicy grilled chicken. Once you know how to make the marinade you can use it for fish or meat. It's great for barbecues.

Feeds 6.
Preparation time: 15 minutes plus overnight marinating.
Cooking time:10 minutes.
You will need:

▓ 12 skinned boned chicken thighs or 6 skinned, boneless chicken breasts, cut into 2.5cm/1in squares if you are using skewers

For the marinade

▓ 1 teaspoon ground coriander
▓ 1 teaspoon ground cumin
▓ 2.5cm/1in fresh ginger, peeled and grated
▓ 2 garlic cloves, crushed
▓ 2 teaspoons paprika
▓ juice of half a lemon
▓ 150ml/5fl oz creamy natural yoghurt.

1. First make the marinade: mix all the ingredients together in a bowl. Place the chicken in a dish and pour over the mixture. Cover and place in the fridge overnight.
2. Heat the grill to high. Thread the chicken pieces onto skewers (if you don't have any it doesn't matter) and then grill for 8–10 minutes, ensuring that the chicken is cooked on all sides. Baste the cubes from time to time with the marinade.

Hint: Line the grill with foil – reduces washing up or covers up yesterday's burnt morsels.

Lamb and Coconut Curry

Feeds 6–8.
This is only for serious curry lovers – it's the real McCoy.
Preparation time: 30 minutes.
Cooking time: 1 hour.
You will need:

- 3 tablespoons vegetable oil
- 2 onions, chopped
- 2 cloves of garlic, chopped
- 900g/2lb stewing lamb, cut into cubes
- 325g/14oz can of tomatoes, chopped
- 3 potatoes, peeled and cubed
- 1 teaspoon salt
- 180ml/6oz coconut milk.

For the curry paste

- 2 teaspoons ground cumin
- 2 teaspoons ground coriander
- 2 dried chillies, finely chopped
- quarter teaspoon mustard seeds
- half teaspoon ground turmeric
- half teaspoon ground fenugreek
- half teaspoon cinnamon
- freshly ground black pepper
- 2 tablespoons white malt vinegar.

1. To make the curry paste, the first thing you have to do is to toast the spices to release the flavours: Heat the cumin, coriander, chillies, mustard seeds, turmeric, fenugreek, cinnamon and black pepper in a frying-pan (preferably cast-iron but let's be realistic!). Cook over a gentle heat for 5 minutes, stirring all the time and ensuring that they do not burn. Remove from the heat, stir in the vinegar and then transfer the paste to a little bowl.
2. Heat the oil in a saucepan, add the onions and garlic and fry for 5 minutes. Stir in the curry paste and cook for a further 3 minutes.
3. Add the lamb and fry in the spice mixture for 6 minutes. Stir in the tomatoes and bring to the boil. Reduce the heat to low, cover the pan and simmer for 40 minutes, stirring from time to time.
4. After 40 minutes add the potatoes, salt and coconut milk and bring to the boil. Once again, lower the heat and simmer for 10 minutes, or until the potatoes are cooked. Serve with rice and lager.

Warning: your flat may smell like 'The Moon of India' tandoori for a few weeks. Make sure your flatmates like curry.

Dal

Feeds 4.

Dal can be made using red, green or yellow lentils or split peas. It is a delicious and wholesome dish for vegetarians as well as being a great accompaniment for other curries.

Preparation time: 10 minutes.
Cooking time: 1 hour 20 minutes.
You will need:

- 3 tablespoons vegetable oil
- 3 garlic cloves, chopped
- 2 medium onions, chopped
- half teaspoon ground cumin
- 225g/8oz lentils, rinsed
- quarter teaspoon cayenne powder
- 1l/1.5pt vegetable stock, made with 3 cubes
- half teaspoon ground turmeric
- salt and pepper.

1. In a large casserole, heat the oil and add the garlic, onion and cumin. Cook for 5 minutes until golden brown.
2. Add the lentils and the vegetable stock. Stir around, bring to the boil, turn the heat down very low and simmer for 1 hour. Stir occasionally to avoid sticking.
3. Stir in the cayenne, salt and pepper and simmer for a further 8 minutes.

Tip: you could bake this in the oven, in which case you could go to the pub or library for an hour. Substitute stage 2 for 1 hour at 190C/375F.

Vegetarian Curry

This is another excellent way of using up tired vegetables. It is especially good if you use lots of root vegetables as the main ingredients. Make it in a wok.

Feeds 4–6.
Preparation time: 20 minutes.
Cooking time: 45 minutes.
You will need:

- 4 tablespoons vegetable oil or ghee
- 1kg/2.2lbs root vegetables (potato, sweet potato, carrots, parsnips etc) Peeled, washed and chopped into 4cm/1.5in cubes, plus any salvaged vegetables from fridge – anything will do, just prepare them normally
- 2 large onions, diced
- 8 garlic cloves, chopped
- 2 teaspoons cumin seeds, toasted
- 1 teaspoon ground coriander
- 1 teaspoon ground turmeric
- half teaspoon Cayenne pepper
- 2 tins coconut milk
- 1 teaspoon garam masala
- 2 tablespoons fresh coriander, coarsely chopped (optional garnish).

1. Heat the oil or ghee in the wok and add the root vegetables. Stir them around occasionally and cook for 10 minutes until they are browned all over.
2. Add the onion, garlic, cumin seeds, ground coriander, turmeric and cayenne and continue stirring gently (try not to break up the root veggies) for another 5 minutes.
3. Now throw in the rest of your salvaged vegetables and pour in the coconut milk. Bring up to the boil and simmer covered for 20 minutes. If it starts to get too dry add a little boiling water.
4. Uncover, stir in garam masala and garnish with chopped coriander. Serve with plain rice.

Index

Index of Recipes

(V) are vegetarian dishes

Index of Advertisers